Against the Herd

Against the Herd

6 Contrarian Investment Strategies You Should Follow

Steve Cortés

WILEY

John Wiley & Sons, Inc.

Published by John Wiley & Sons, Inc., Hoboken, New Jersey.
Published simultaneously in Canada.

For general information on our other products and services or for technical support,
please contact our Customer Care Department within the United States at (800)
762–2974, outside the United States at (317) 572–3993 or fax (317) 572–4002.

Wiley also publishes its books in a variety of electronic formats. Some content that
appears in print may not be available in electronic books. For more information about
Wiley products, visit our web site at www.wiley.com.

Library of Congress Cataloging-in-Publication Data:
Cortés, Steve, 1972–
    Against the herd: 6 contrarian investment strategies you should follow / Steve
Cortés.—1
      p. cm.
    Includes index.
    ISBN 978-1-118-08318-5 (cloth); ISBN 978-1-118-20585-3 (ebk);
    ISBN 978-1-118-20586-0 (ebk); ISBN 978-1-118-20584-6 (ebk)
      1. Investments. I. Title.
    [DNLM: 1. Economic history—21st century.]
  HG4515.C67 2011
  332.6—dc23

                                                                    2011035471

Printed in the United States of America
10 9 8 7 6 5 4 3 2 1

Contents

Against the Herd

Introduction

"*Safety in numbers.*"

That phrase, and that concept, are deeply imbedded in our human psyche. We are clearly social creatures, hard-wired to desire companionship in all its wonderful forms, for benefits both tangible and intangible. Indeed, modern life is largely marked by the constant need for connectivity to each other. The incredible success of Facebook and Google+, and the constant inclination to text and instant message all speak to this yearning for the collective, for connectivity.

But safety in numbers can be illusory. Is the crowd to be followed, or feared? Twitter can inform and enlighten and also form dangerous riots and "flash mobs." Should we cast a skeptical eye upon the supposed wisdom of the masses? In this digital age, mass opinions form quickly and powerfully, but often with little connection to reality, especially concerning economics and markets. For many investors, financial market analysis properly lies well down their list of priorities, behind family, career, and community. But that lack of market acumen

1

often leaves investors all too willing to accept the conventional wisdom thrust upon them by Wall Street and the financial media. Therefore, maintaining a healthy skepticism becomes paramount to protecting and growing assets. A willingness to think independently forms the backbone of a stable financial life. Moreover, the contrarian thinker must always scour the market landscape for unrecognized risks, for those instances when the masses have whipped themselves into frenzied, widely held, but dangerous beliefs—such as the dot-com bubble of 1999–2000.

As a trader and market researcher, I am constantly searching for just those kinds of risks, which can become opportunities. I look for those instances when conventional wisdom misses the mark, setting us up for an eventual economic reckoning. The subprime housing fiasco represented just such a chasm between accepted opinion and underlying reality. This book is designed to target unrecognized dangers and help you avoid financial pain, if not actually profit from such dangers.

Casting a Fresh Eye on the World Around You

Danger is often found where one least suspects it. And profit is often found in equally unlikely places. For example, if one is asked, "What is the greatest casualty disaster in Chicago history?" most people, even most Chicagoans, would respond "the Chicago Fire." In fact, the greatest loss of life—and one of the worst maritime disasters in U.S. history—occurred in a mass drowning in 20 feet of calm water in the Chicago River.

On July 24, 1915, the workers and families of a Western Electric plant in Cicero, Illinois, eagerly anticipated a summertime boat ride out to the beaches of northern Indiana and a company-sponsored picnic. For these working class laborers, mostly Czech immigrants, such diversions were rare and much appreciated. But the SS Eastland, the ship selected to transport about 2,700 of the workers and families that fateful morning, already held a spotty safety record. It was simply built too tall and too top-heavy for its structure and was, therefore, prone to listing. Near disasters in past voyages had failed to deter the *Eastland* from staying in service. In fact, as is often the case, government intervention only exacerbated the problem. Specifically, in 1915 the Seaman's Act passed Congress; it was a reaction to the *Titanic* tragedy of 1912. The Act required a vastly increased number of lifeboats on large ships, and the added weight on the *Eastland* greatly augmented the dangers of its already flawed design.

Ignorant of the design flaws of this vessel, almost 3,000 passengers boarded the *Eastland*. As if choreographed, the workers and families crowded herd-like, seemingly all at once, onto the top deck's far port side. Their collective weight capsized the ship into the river, trapping hundreds of passengers under the boat itself and below deck as the boat filled with water. In total, 844 people drowned—in only 20 feet of water and mere yards away from the dock. Jack Woodford of the *Herald and Examiner* newspaper wrote:

As I watched in disoriented stupefaction a steamer large as an ocean liner slowly turned over on its side as though it were a whale going to take a nap. I didn't believe a huge steamer had done this before my eyes, lashed to a dock, in perfectly calm water, in excellent weather, with no explosion, no fire, nothing. I thought I had gone crazy.[1]

We ascertain two important lessons from this dreadful tale.

- First, danger is seldom most acute in the most obvious places. Often the bathtub of water presents more danger than furious seas. For example, home mortgages, the stuff of the Bailey Building and Loan in the movie *It's a Wonderful Life*, had served for decades as the dependable, and even boring, basis of our "ownership society."
- Second, following the herd can be very costly. When masses of people decide assuredly on an opinion, history (and the history

of markets) argues to take caution, because the madness and delusions of the crowd can create dangerous and untenable scenarios that imperil all but the most independent thinkers.

More than for any other purpose, I write this book hoping it will empower the reader to wisely discern the motivations of the media and Wall Street, and to realize how important it is to truly *think*. "Think" was the one-word motto of Thomas Watson of IBM, one of history's greatest capitalists, whom I will describe later in the final chapter. A failure to think cost too many people far too much hard-earned money during the recent credit crisis. Following the herd proved disastrous and provided no safety in numbers but rather incredible risks.

A willingness to think, as Thomas Watson did, requires the courage to be different, given our internal need for connectivity, our inclination tends toward conformity, toward getting along. But the contrarian investor must develop the mindset of a maverick, a willingness to think and act in unpopular ways. The term maverick itself emanates from just such a man, Samuel Augustus Maverick, a Texan (naturally) who, in the nineteenth century, found fortune as a land baron after fighting in the Texas revolution against Mexico. He refused to brand his cattle, which was the convention. His claimed motivation was to spare the cattle the pain of the hot iron, although some speculated he actually wanted the ability to claim all unbranded roaming cattle as his own. Regardless of his reasons, Sam Maverick was unafraid to be different. And thus his name was introduced into our American lexicon to describe a person willing to live unconventionally.

It's worth mentioning here, though, that not every popular or unanimous mass opinion is wrong. For example, when the United States sent the Dream Team to the Barcelona Olympics in 1992 to reclaim American basketball glory, it was uniformly assumed that Jordan, Barkley, Bird, and Ewing would smash all opposition. The Dream Team did so triumphantly, claiming the gold for U.S. basketball and winning by an average of 43 points per game. Clearly, at times the masses are correct. But just as often, when popular opinion, media attention, and Wall Street analysts all combine to form a universally acknowledged economic "truth," it often pays to recall, as I was once told by a cynical but streetwise teller at a Las Vegas sports book, "Kid, the masses are asses." So while it's important to resist the label of contrarian simply for the sake of the moniker, so too is it vital to think independently, to use the myriad resources now available to anyone willing to think independently, to do his or her homework, and search for unconventional opportunities.

The contrarian thinker is not some grumpy argumentative type, always saying "no," but rather an adventurous, independent thinker, trying to discern the reality of the world of economics, rather than just following the herd's thinking. Later in this book, I will present Dr. Michael Burry, made famous by Michael Lewis's book, *The Big Short*, which detailed how one man doing serious homework made a fortune for himself and his investors by betting against the excesses of the subprime lending crisis. I will also detail why I think China is so dangerous now and presents a risk to the global economy as severe as the subprime fiasco. As in the case of subprime, finding skeptics about the whole emerging market theme today is not easy. Wall Street and the financial media badly want us to believe that the future lies in places like Shanghai, Bombay, and Abu Dhabi. Of all the most widely held investment beliefs right now, to me the most false by far is the belief that the future belongs to the emerging markets and that America's economic supremacy is receding. Quite to the contrary, I see massive risks in emerging markets, which may soon become submerging markets. Long term, I foresee boundless opportunities in the United States, which I believe shall remain for many decades the world's sole superpower in every facet of life—economically, culturally, militarily, politically.

What You'll Find in This Book

To paraphrase Mark Twain, history might not repeat, but it sure seems to rhyme. Bubbles unfold when the masses decide, often at the behest of the self-interested intelligentsia, that a new order or paradigm is unassailable. I see such thinking currently enveloping the near hysteria surrounding China and its potential, a tale darkly reminiscent of Japan in the 1980s, which will be discussed in Chapter 2. Only a confident, independent, and rigorous thinker can discern when the masses have ventured beyond the reasonable realm of risk and reward. Whether deciding in 1915 to stay lonely on the starboard side of the *SS Eastland*, or in 2011 to refrain from betting on the Chinese "miracle" (or, in fact, bet against it!), contrarian, independent analysis can, at least, protect capital and, at best, build profit.

This book will also detail the lingering risks that abound in housing and stipulate that, far from being at an assured bottom in prices, housing will languish for years ahead. Given the turbulence of markets in recent years, the natural inclination to hold gold as an investment has grown wildly. On television lately, gold commercials have started to eclipse even the volume of Viagra advertisements. But is the yellow metal a legitimate long-term investment, or a fool's gold? I believe the latter, and I will lay out the endemic risks in gold. Much of this book bucks the conventional wisdom of Wall Street, which may serve well the interests of the Street but not of the average investor. Nowhere is that gulf more evident than when we scrutinize Wall Street's typical asset allocation blend. I will make the case that most investors own far too many stocks and cannot handle the incredible volatility that is actually inherent to stock investing.

So I ask that you join me on a global investing adventure and consider where the herd has gotten the story wrong. More than anything, I ask you to think, and in doing so, develop a healthy skepticism toward mass opinion, especially in the realm of financial markets. Thinking independently, developing a healthy skepticism, and acting like a maverick investor, one willing to buck the movement of the herd, can evolve into an exhilarating, secure, and profitable financial existence.

Chapter 1

The Corleones Meet Confucius

The Chinese Mirage of Miracle Expansion

In *The Godfather II*, Michael Corleone consults his advisers in his Lake Tahoe mansion following an unsuccessful assassination attempt against him. The young, powerful Don Corleone considers the likelihood of insider help in the plot, from within the Corleone family organization. Michael counsels:

All our people's loyalty is based on business; and on that basis, anything is possible.

Whether a crime family, a company, or an ordinary family, if the organization's central binding ethos is money, then the flow of capital must not cease or the organization splinters quickly. It is not an absurd analogy to compare the motivations of the members of the Corleone family to the majority of the citizens of China. That is, like the Corleones, China is not truly a family. It is not even truly a country. Instead, China is more like a group of countries—a vast collection of disparate, and often confrontational, cultures, languages, and histories. And since the reforms of Deng Xiaoping, the glue that binds the amalgam together is not ideology but commerce. George Friedman, political scientist and founder of the private intelligence corporation Stratfor, correctly postulates:

China is held together by money, not ideology. When there is an economic downturn and the money stops rolling in, not only will the banking system spasm, but the entire fabric of Chinese society will shudder. Loyalty in China is either bought or coerced. Without available money, only coercion remains.[1]

Like the Corleones, the Communist Party that controls China faces a daunting task: trying to purchase the loyalty of the Chinese masses. Consider that the Party must simultaneously balance China's fierce pace of growth, manage the world's largest-ever migration of people (from western China to the coast), steer all industrial policy, and—perhaps most dauntingly—allocate capital effectively. And the Party must manage these myriad tasks while maintaining a system of tyrannical oppression of thought, communication, religion, assembly, and even reproduction.

That repression should soon become far more apparent, once the flow of credit slows. Already, Chinese authorities are quickly tightening monetary policy—that is, restricting the availability of credit—to stem the impending threat of food inflation that imperils the still-poor masses, especially in the western interior lands. As credit recedes, coercion must rise, otherwise Beijing relinquishes control. As Michael Corleone knew, when buying loyalty becomes impractical, force becomes indispensable. Corleone had his henchmen; the Chinese have the People's Liberation Army.

In this chapter, I detail the inherent contradictions and attendant dangers endemic to China as presently structured. Further, I make the case that China's fierce expansion is unsustainable, representing an economic mirage, analogous to Japan of the 1980s and a similarly dangerous investment. I maintain that, far from presenting a credible threat to American supremacy, China will in fact be fortunate to even maintain itself as a unified state.

Exposing the Myth

Despite the myriad risks relevant to China, it represents perhaps the most widely held fallacy of our age. The herd is, indeed, stampeding into China. Western companies and western capital flow torrent-like into the Middle Kingdom, ignorant of Chinese history (and Japanese recent history) and cavalier about partnering with Beijing. Instead, the West beholds a near-unanimous belief that China is an unstoppable force of progress and modernization, an economic miracle before our eyes. Moreover, asserts conventional wisdom, China will soon threaten, and assuredly surpass, the economic, political, and military primacy of the United States. In fact, many on Wall Street expect that growth in China will miraculously lead the global recovery out of the depths of the credit crisis of 2008. Instead, I assert that China presents the most stark single risk to the global recovery. Far from being a locomotive leading a global resurgence, China instead hangs like a Sword of Damocles over the world economy.

But, rather strikingly, the bullish view on all things Chinese traverses wide swaths of our society. The vision of China that has been successfully sold to the American public by the media and Wall Street is a carefully orchestrated, well-honed machine with brilliant top-down control emanating from the allegedly wise, forward-looking leaders in Beijing. In this mien, we Americans supposedly look foolish by comparison, with our diffused and democratic power structures. America is inefficient, goes the thinking, while China presents a model of twenty-first century progress through a controlled, almost scientific approach.

In reality, a better analog for comparison is not some well-oiled machine, but instead a wild, dangerous bucking bull. And Party leaders in Beijing, in stark contrast to the image of wise, measured seers, are instead like a cowboy riding a bull, losing control but desperately trying to stay on. Bull riding is a sport far better reserved to American cowboys than Chinese leaders, and the bull that is China's internal situation will soon buck the rider into a painful dismount. Nevertheless, from Wall Street research departments to Ivy League academies to Main Street, the assurance of China's ascendancy reigns nearly unchallenged.

The Gallup Poll asked Americans, "What country has the world's largest economy?" In 2009, respondents placed America and China at a tie. In February 2011, an amazing 52 percent of Americans named China as the largest economy in the world, with only 32 percent naming the United States.[2]

In reality, America is, by a giant margin, the largest economy. According to the International Monetary Fund, the 2010 GDP of the United States was $14.62 trillion, compared to China's $5.75 trillion. Further, given China's far larger population, the per capita gap is even starker, with China's per-person GDP at $4,000 versus America's $47,000.

Lately, when watching business television, talking to economic consultants, or reading the financial media, it has become rare to hear anything but almost reverential descriptions of China. In fact, analysts trip over themselves competing to make even grander predictions about China's potential and growth. The seduction of the simplicity of top-down, command economy is presently capturing the imagination—and the capital—of much of America's elite.

A similar movement occurred in the 1980s when Japan was, according to the American media and cognoscenti, about to economically swallow up the United States. Instead, Japan now finds itself staring at a third consecutive lost decade, as we examine in the next chapter. But while history may not repeat, it sure seems to rhyme. Today, what multinational company CEO does not pin his growth strategy on emerging markets in general, and on China specifically? The chorus is loud and far too self-assured about China's growth prospects.

As an example, I recently went to a dinner attended by large asset managers in New York City at Sparks Steakhouse, a popular restaurant for traders and bankers in midtown Manhattan. As we dug into very American-sized giant steaks, the China praise was effusive. Of the six men seated at the table, I was literally the *only* one whose children were not taking Mandarin! When a wave becomes that unanimous, we're surely on the edge of sustainability. I modestly suggested that perhaps Spanish would represent a much more important language for America, given our southern border and the demographic trends within America itself. My suggestion was met with polite but dismissive interest.

We will examine later in the book why Americans (and Westerners broadly) mistakenly so fear and respect China. But first, it's vital to examine the growth-killing hurdles facing China.

Adam Smith's Revenge: The Folly of Central Planning

In *The Wealth of Nations*, Adam Smith extolled the wondrous, surprising harmony of the "invisible hand," the collection of millions of individuals, businesses, and interests naturally aligning into efficient channels of commerce, spurred by the dynamic forces of supply and demand, and compelled to creative action by the profit motive. He warned against central planning, the idea that government can and should determine an overarching economic policy for a country, and insert policy into the affairs of commerce. Instead, he argued for the unpredictable elegance, the surprising harmony of a society's combined collective genius, propelled by countless individuals acting in self-interest. His warnings to politicians arrogant enough to attempt to manage the affairs of millions stands the test of time, and it powerfully indicts the Chinese Communist Party bosses of 2011. He warned against central planning, which he described as:

The statesman who should attempt to direct private people in what manner they ought to employ their capitals, would not only load himself with a most unnecessary attention, but assume an authority which could safely be trusted, not only to no single person, but to no council or senate whatever, and which would nowhere be so dangerous as in the hands of a man who had folly and presumption enough to fancy himself fit to exercise it.[3]

Regarding Adam Smith, hedge fund titan and China bear Jim Chanos noted on CNBC: "Adam Smith is going to get his revenge in China."[4]

Despite endless examples of the folly of central planning—from Stalinist Russia to 1980s Japan to the U.S. government's mortgage agency debacles—politicians, media, and investors continue to fall for the alluring myth of central planning. Human nature seems almost perversely drawn to such schemes, wanting badly to believe that councils of wise men can effectively direct economies and whole societies. Resisting this temptation, and standing aside of, or even against, the herd can be lonely, but also safe and profitable. For example, not following the crowd onto one side of the deck of the *SS Eastland* would have precluded personal disaster.

In the case of China, the herd, after all, is ignoring voluminous historical evidence to the contrary, and betting massively that the Party in Beijing can, in the face of history and against all principles of free markets, hit a hole-in-one and successfully commandeer a statist, quasi-capitalist economy of 1.3 billion people. Such an autocratic approach to money and markets leads, inevitably, not to sustainable growth and lasting wealth, but rather to cronyism, bubbles, and severe misallocations of capital.

In fact, China appears to be moving even more forcefully toward state control, emphasizing (unsurprisingly) its state-controlled businesses now that the global economy has so slowed. Michael Wines noted in the *New York Times*:

Once eager to learn from the United States, China's leaders during the financial crisis have reaffirmed their faith in their own more statist approach to economic management, in which private capitalism plays only a supporting role.[5]

In fact, of the 100 largest publicly traded Chinese companies, a grand total of *one* is not majority owned by the state. In an even more brazen display of cronyism, of the 129 major state enterprises, more than half of the chairmen were appointed by the Communist Party.[6] Can any investor honestly believe that those appointments are based primarily on merit?

The very definition of capitalism is the *private allocation of capital*. So in reality, China's economic model is not capitalism at all, but rather a command economy attempting to meet the supply/demand needs of other capitalist economies. The capitalist aspects of Chinese society, therefore, are not free or fair, but instead represent, in the words of eminent Chinese economist Wu Jinglian, "capitalism of the rich and powerful."[7]

Such cronyism naturally leads to ineffective resource allocations. For example, China keeps on massively investing in auto production despite the fact that, at present, global auto production capacity stands at 86 million vehicles per year, with present projects expected to expand that capacity to 100 million by 2015. And yet, presently the world is only buying about 55 million new vehicles per year.[8]

And how about bridges for those cars? Apparently bridge builders in China operate a very effective political action committee. Consider that the United States, roughly the geographic size of China, maintains 450,000 usable bridges. By comparison, China presently has 500,000 bridges, after building 15,000 per annum for the past 10 years, even though the United States has *five times* more rivers than China. And the United States has *five times* more cars than China. And already China has a comparable number of expressways to that of the United States.[9]

Speaking of bridges, there was in July 2011 a truly tragic accident in Wenzhou in eastern China, in which two high-speed trains collided near a bridge over the Ou River, killing 40 people and hospitalizing 192 more. The crash was, I believe, perhaps symptomatic of the dangers of such rapid, top-down directed industrialization. Even more telling, though, was the Chinese official response to the disaster. Rather than conduct an open, serious inquiry into the causes of the tragedy, the Chinese government quite literally buried large portions of the train carriages, thereby preventing any real forensic type of analysis. This reaction stands in utter contrast to the reaction to tragedies in the West. Granted, America's obsession with litigation would have likely meant trial lawyers at the site concurrent with paramedics; this is an unwelcome reality of American life. But on the very positive side, had the accident occurred in the United States, the analysis of its causes and possible preventions would be thoroughly, openly evaluated.

But in China, the first priority of the government is never the safety of the people; instead the goal is growth, and growth at all costs. The need, therefore, for endless Biblically sized infrastructure projects in China, based on capacity and real demand, becomes spurious. But the political need for such projects, to employ the migrating masses and line the pockets of connected interests, is undeniable—and dangerous.

Ghost Cities and Construction Cranes

One rather frightening place those cars and bridges can reach is the Ghost City of Ordos. The original old Ordos lies on top of one-sixth of all the coal reserves of China. So despite its remote location near the Mongolian border, Ordos prospered. Its citizens produced about three times the national average GDP of China, ranking it only behind Shanghai and ahead of Beijing. Ordos became known as China's Texas.

But, unsatisfied with its natural resource-based achievements, the Party determined that a massive planned city, a "new Ordos City," must spring up from the desert. So 30 minutes away from the old Ordos, a giant monument to the folly of central planning emerged:

The Kangbashi district began as a public-works project in Ordos, a wealthy coal-mining town in Inner Mongolia. The area is filled with office towers, administrative centers, government buildings, museums, theaters and sports fields—not to mention acre on acre of subdivisions overflowing with middle-class duplexes and bungalows. The only problem: the district was originally designed to house, support and entertain 1 million people, yet hardly anyone lives there.[10]

But Ordos (shown in Figure 1.1), while notable for its massive scale, does not at all represent an exceptional story of following the Chinese model. Rather, bridges to nowhere and ghost towns are quickly becoming the norm as China struggles to spend its massive $585 billion stimulus. That stimulus, by the way, compared to the size of China's economy, dwarfs America's similarly ill-conceived attempts at stimulus. But in the Chinese version, GDP becomes not the result of a vibrant model but instead the very model itself. That is, growth, at any cost, and in spite of any waste and irrespective of profit margins, becomes the overarching goal. Cash flow, not profits, becomes king. Because, like the Corleones, Beijing needs to purchase the peace.

A more bizarre ghost city has sprung up much nearer to Shanghai, called Thames Town. Built to replicate a British country village, Thames Town looks eerily like a theme park homage to Britain, complete with a replica church and fish and chips shop. The only problem is that, similar to Ordos, no one lives there. The quaint English village is empty.

Tadashi Nakamae, perhaps Japan's preeminent global strategist, has endured a front-seat view of the failures of Japan's central planning. Nakamae specifically cites the massive overcapacity of industrial production in China. More frighteningly, he posits that China continues

Figure 1.1   Ghost City of Ordos
Source: Huai-Chun Hsu.

to expand capacity, even though final demand is slowing, internally and internationally. But again, the Chinese manager answers not to an American-style board or investor base but, in reality, to the Chinese government. He surmises that China will "continue down the reckless path of adding capacity by mass overproduction not driven by market demand but by administrative edict."[11]

Such administrative edict created an Ordos-like boondoggle much further south of Mongolia—the New South China Mall in Dongguan on the southeast Chinese coast (see Figure 1.2). It stands as the largest mall in the world, with capacity for an astonishing 2,350 stores and a replica of the Arc de Triomphe. But the New South China Mall is also notable for something embarrassing: It is 99 percent empty.

Figure 1.2 But Where Are All the Shoppers?

Just before the mall debuted, the *New York Times*, in hagiographic praise all too common from the Western press, hailed the Mall as proof of China's "astonishing new consumer culture" and noted "there is no end in sight—and no evidence that China's long boom is likely to suffer anything more than a modest slowdown."[12]

Instead of "no end in sight" inside the mall, there are in fact, no *people* in sight—no shoppers, no workers. Indeed, China now claims 7 of the 10 largest malls in the world. But one stark, remarkably inconvenient truth remains: that Chinese consumers represent only 36 percent of GDP. Compared to the 50+ percent for India and 71 percent for the United States,[13] can this relatively small consumer appetite really satiate the über-ambitious plans of the Chinese government?

But despite the obvious failures of projects like Ordos and the New South China Mall, the pace of construction, at the behest of the government, actually quickens monthly. At present fixed asset investment represents an almost unbelievable 70 percent of GDP. By comparison, at its peak, U.S. construction only comprised 16 percent of GDP.[14] For this reason, Jim Chanos labeled China "Dubai times 1000."[15] At its peak, Dubai saw 240 square meters of property development for every $1 million in GDP. In urban China presently, the ratio is four times as high. Chanos expounds, "We've seen this movie before." From Dubai to Thailand during the Asian crisis of the late 1990s, to Tokyo circa 1989, "this always ends badly."[16]

And the evidence mounts that Chinese real estate valuations have reached unsustainable levels. For example, housing prices in the United States peaked nationally at 6.4 times average annual earnings. In Beijing, the present multiple is 22 times. In prestige cities like London and Los Angeles, the figure in 2007 at the highs never exceeded 10 times, yet Shenzhen housing presently trades at 25 times.[17]

As further evidence of the massive infrastructure bubble—despite a global glut of capacity, after financial crisis—consider China's present cement consumption. China produces more cement than the rest of the world's countries combined. Its estimated spare capacity exceeds the total cement production of India, the United States, and Japan combined. And perhaps most telling, proportionally it's now consuming roughly the same amount of cement per person as Ireland and Spain in recent years—countries that were poster children for excessive construction bubbles.[18]

Global companies have been far too willing to jump headfirst into the warm waters of Chinese expansion. For example, Vale, the giant Brazilian iron ore producer, boasted that because of Chinese demand, it now commands the second largest fleet of ships on earth, outside of the U.S. Navy.[19]

Consequently, global investors need to avoid, or short, companies with too high an exposure to Chinese construction and real estate. For example, global metals, shipping, and steel names all appear vulnerable to the inevitable retrenchment in Chinese construction. Especially dangerous are companies with a heavy Asian-Pacific emphasis, such as

Australian metals play BHP Billiton, the American Union Pacific railroad with its heavy dependence on west coast United States to Asia transit, and the aforementioned Brazilian giant, and surface competitor to the U.S. Navy, Vale.

China Too Crowded? Not for Long . . .

One reason the pace and scope of construction are untenable is that China has a serious population problem. Only, it's not the population problem the world expects. The actual, undeniable problem is not that China will have too many people, but rather *too few*. To be more specific, there will be too few young people. And of particular importance, there will be precariously too few young women.

The disastrous decades-long one-child policy, combined with increased longevity, has induced an aging of the Chinese population that stands unprecedented in history. For example, China first reached 1.2 billion people in 1994. Twelve years later in 2006 it hit 1.3 billion. Adding another 100 million people, to reach 1.4 billion, will take an estimated 20 years from then, until 2026, when China's population will peak and start descending.[20] Even worse, because of rapid aging, the labor supply of China will peak in 2017.[21]

The population will peak, because of declining birth rates, well below population replenishment. In 1990, Chinese women averaged an above-replacement 2.2 births. By 1995, that average fell to 1.8 births per woman. Today, the average Chinese woman has a fertility rate of only 1.6. The migration of hundreds of millions of people has sparked far lower reproduction. First, because in urban factory lifestyles, children become an economic burden, as opposed to rural subsistence farming where children provide valuable, free assistance. And second, because this mass migration has also separated literally millions of families, with one or both parents living near the coast working, while children (usually child, in the singular) reside in the peasant west, often in the care of grandparents. As evidenced by Figure 1.3, families spread

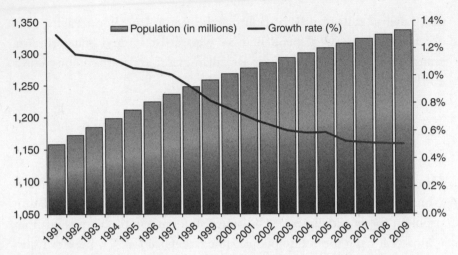

Figure 1.3 China's Population Trends and Growth Rate, 1991 to 2009
SOURCE: Starmass International.

across China are simply not having multiple children, as romantic as the prospect of industrial dormitory residences might seem.

In contrast, the United States still averages more than 2.1 births per woman and, combined with steady immigration, keeps the total U.S. population growing far into the future. China's National Population and Family Planning Commission claims to have prevented 400 million births through the one-child policy. The Commission is now reversing itself and allowing second births in five provinces. This new policy is expected to be rolled out nationwide by 2014.[22]

But demographics are troublesome. Once births decline precipitously, the problem becomes quite literally terminal; that is, reversing the aging, declining population would require multiple births per woman on a scale beyond reasonable probability.

This decline in births and coming dearth of young workers arrives at a most inopportune time. China has thrived for a decade on the mass influx of migrant, cheap labor from the interior west of the country, but since 2005 this flow of eager, cheap labor is declining. Credit Suisse notes in its 2011 report "China: Turning Point of the Labour Market" that "in 2010, factories suddenly noticed that it had become much harder to find workers, and a 30 to 40 percent salary increase was almost a must if they were to have any chance of capturing those still interested in working in the coastal areas." China has not prospered through creativity and innovation, as we will examine in coming pages. Instead, it has seen rapid growth as the world's factory and smelter. It has become the toy factory for every Wal-Mart shelf in the United States and a low-end foundry for India. But China's greatest asset—abundant, cheap labor—is dissipating as it reaches the "Lewis point" where the surplus of agricultural labor tapers off. The Lewis Turning Point was first expounded on by Sir Arthur Lewis, a Nobel laureate economist who concluded that developed countries see fast wage growth once the free flow of workers from the countryside to the city's industrial centers abates.[23] As evidence of China reaching the Lewis point, executive Bob Rice of the U.S.-based Master Lock Company recently stated that, because of rising Chinese wages and inferior productivity, "I can manufacture combination locks in Milwaukee for less of a cost than I can in China."[24] Years of rising wages have taken a toll and eliminated the only real Chinese advantage, which was seemingly endless cheap labor. Goldman Sachs's chief economist in Hong Kong, Helen Qiao, points out that, for a full decade, real wages in China have advanced on average 12 percent per year.[25]

The demographics, meaning fewer young, productive, affordable workers, guarantee that China will continue to lose this comparative advantage. And more broadly, such a decline in the young, productive segment of any society will surely restrain growth going forward, whether in China or elsewhere. If the past is prologue, which it normally is, then China is in for particular trouble. The Chinese baby boomers (born 1955 to 1965) have closely matched the "footprint of the Chinese economy—the production boom of the 1990s, the housing boom of the 2000s and the recent consumption boom."[26] But as this bulge of boomers enters their fifties and the one-child generation ascends, Chinese growth will recede, especially compared to the United States.

Accordingly, investors will, in coming years, be well advised to avoid multinationals that bet too heavily on the much anticipated enormous Chinese consumer class. Specifically, consumer discretionary names, particularly those with an Asian focus, should be avoided— or shorted. Companies like Tiffany and Coach should be especially burdened. The herd is promising a market in scope and depth that will dwarf the U.S. consumer appetite. But such promises ignore the harsh realities of Chinese demographics. When I was young my mother warned me against doing dumb things simply because the crowd was doing it, especially the cool kids. Similarly, capital will be wise to avoid too much Chinese exposure just because Tiffany and Coach promise a yellow brick road (or Chinese Wall) to riches. In point of fact, China's consumer appetite is actually declining as a percentage of its GDP, and rather precipitously so. As China ages and the Chinese save ever more, mindful of a dearth of social programs for the elderly, the long-promised mass Chinese consumer market becomes far less likely. Specifically, for 2010 the consumer made up only 36 percent of total Chinese GDP, the lowest on record since the market reforms 30 years ago, and off from 46 percent just 10 years ago.[27]

China is not, of course, alone among nations in facing a declining and aging population. Italy, Spain, Russia, and especially Japan face similar, if not worse, scenarios. But compared to the United States, which stands alone among industrial societies growing in numbers, China represents a poor investment. We will discuss this key advantage of America much more in the final chapter. But suffice it to point out that investments are based on growth—growth of incomes, numerical population growth. China's population is about to crest, meaning that growth is already tapering off and will soon result in outright declines in the number of people. Such a recession of people does not bode well for long-term capital growth.

One final point on demographics: The male/female mismatch represents a truly unprecedented, and perhaps very volatile, wild card in analyzing the future of China. Due to the one-child policy and mass abortions of girls, the ratio of male to female births has climbed to 119 to 100. In some rural provinces, the ratio is 130 to 100.[28]

If I am even partially correct about a Chinese economic slow-down, what ramifications will result from this macro gender imbalance? In general, this book seeks to use the lessons of history to gain some reasonable divination of future trends. For example, studying Chinese history reveals the fissures among the ethnic groups that make up China. And similarly, studying 1980s Japan (which we will examine in Chapter 2) provides an analog for the command cash-flow-centered economy of present-day China. But there is literally no comparison for this present Chinese gender imbalance. Many societies have witnessed a dearth of males, especially following brutal wars, but a dearth of young women? If the economy does splinter, what will become of young, unattached, unemployed men? The honest answer is "I don't know," but I doubt the outcome will be pleasant. The idea of undomesticated single males fighting over resources and wives does not engender optimism, but rather suggests a future of strife and instability.

In many years, considering all the missteps of the Chinese government, I suspect that in retrospect this gender imbalance issue will stand out as the most damaging. It may well become a most egregious example of the pernicious unintended consequences of the visible hand of government, especially a government like China's that operates in opacity.

Big Brother's Watching: Censorship and Secrecy

In 1984, the singer Rockwell released his hit song "Somebody's Watching Me" and bemoaned the lack of privacy and concurrent unease at being watched. Well, Rockwell would not enjoy living in China, because Big Brother is indeed watching. For example, recently China's Internet censors filtered and blocked Chinese surfers from

seeing the name of the U.S. Ambassador to China, John Hunts-
man Jr. His offense was appearing, very inconspicuously, as an observer
at a McDonald's gathering of Chinese youth concerned about
human rights.

On the topic of censorship, consider that China has a mind-
boggling 457 million Internet users. Of that total, only an estimated
700,000, or less than 2 percent, use Facebook, which is largely blocked.[29]
Compare that total to the United States, where more than one out of
three Americans (of any age) is on Facebook. And Facebook is hardly
unique. China blocks Google, YouTube, Twitter, and anything it
deems critical of the Communist Party.

The 2010 Nobel Peace Prize winner, Liu Xiaobo, knows all too
well the sting of Chinese censorship. For writings considered subversive
to Beijing, he was arrested in the middle of the night in 2008, tried in
secrecy, and sentenced to 11 years in prison where he sits still, even
after winning the Nobel Prize.

This lack of transparency represents not just an affront to human
rights, but a very real, tangible impediment to a flourishing, lasting
economic growth model. True capitalism requires openness in many
forms. It particularly requires the openness of information, so that actors
can create and capital can seek the best possible allocations. Without
unfiltered information, the process of capital allocation is, at best, inefficient and, at worst, fraught with danger.

Moreover, a culture of secrecy and obfuscation bleeds into commercial sectors as well. For example, recently many Chinese firms
have achieved pseudo-legitimacy by listing shares on the Nasdaq in
the United States. Using a tactic known as a reverse merger, these
companies have bought American shell companies that have a stock
listing but insignificant remaining businesses. After changing the name,
these Chinese firms instantly achieve American publicly traded status.
Since they're foreign firms, the United States allows them to pass
audits in their home country. But what kind of audit standards exist
inside China? Given the utter lack of transparency, and the blatantly
political nature of the Chinese business model, does anyone believe

that the Chinese audits compare well against the standards of the U.S. equivalent?

An example is Fuqi, the Chinese jewelry maker. It is listed on the Nasdaq, trades almost 500,000 shares daily, and at one point boasted a market capitalization value of nearly $1 billion. But in March 2010, Fuqi was forced to admit that it over-reported earnings for 2009 and would have to restate them. As of March 2011, Fuqi still had not filed any new statements and the stock is presently 80 percent off its peak. RINO is a similar story. The Chinese environmental firm was delisted from the Nasdaq after admitting to the SEC that it lied about customer contracts. RINO also secretly lent its CEO $3.5 million, without any loan agreement.[30]

In 2011, a similar but much larger fraud story played out surrounding Sino Forest, a Chinese timber play based in Vancouver, Canada, and traded on the Canadian exchanges. Journalists and investors uncovered huge discrepancies in the amount of land and timber Sino Forest purported to own versus publicly available information from Chinese local governments as well as other forestry companies. Once this alleged fraud was uncovered, the shares predictably careened lower, losing about $750 million for hedge fund titan John Paulson. The China myth, it seems, has taken in even the world's most sophisticated investors. In total, Sino Forest sold about $1 billion in bonds, and insiders sold another $1 billion in shares to investors. With both the shares and bonds close to worthless, hedge fund manager John Hempton notes that Sino Forest represents "probably the largest straight theft in human history."[31]

This lack of transparency endemic to China has already produced serious losses for investors, and undoubtedly the pace and scope of such financial machinations will expand greatly in coming years. Growth covers up myriad problems, misdeeds, and scams. But as the saying goes, "When the tide goes out, you discover who's swimming naked." When Chinese growth slows, as appears to already be happening, then I am convinced the scale and audacity of corporate dishonesty, Party graft, and dirty dealing will truly astound the Western investor.

No H-P Garage

But the worst ramification of the lack of transparency is the concomitant lack of innovation. Creative successes require the fertile soil of openness to grow. Leonardo da Vinci thrived not in a closed society of repression and control, but rather in a Renaissance era abounding in inquiry, fostering a flourishing of commerce, arts, learning, and exploration. The control exerted by Beijing compels just the opposite result: a stifling of creativity and encouragement of conformity.

Even further, this rigid top-down control demands growth at all costs, including flouting internationally recognized protections of intellectual property and copyrights. Consider Zippo, the iconic lighter manufacturer. Since 1937, Zippo has proudly produced its lighters at its only plant in Bradford, Pennsylvania. Every Zippo comes with a lifetime guarantee, "Always works—or we fix it," and for free. The trouble in recent years is that Zippo produces 12 million lighters per year, but receives countless malfunctioning fake lighters for repair (which it won't work on) that have been made in China. Chinese production of "Rippos," as the real company calls the fakes, has reached 12 million per year.

Perhaps more disturbing is China's consistent abrogation and lack of intellectual property standards. For example, the Business Software Alliance, an American industry group that includes Microsoft, Intel, and Apple, said that as of 2008, 80 percent of all software used in China is pirated, costing the industry $6.7 billion in lost revenue. China is the second largest PC market in the world, after the United States, but only the tenth largest PC software market. Regarding counterfeit goods seized by the U.S. Customs and Border Patrol, a General Accounting Office report detailed that from 2004 to 2009, China and Hong King accounted for fully 84 percent of all seized counterfeit goods. For comparison, the next worst offender, India, managed a paltry 2 percent of all seized goods. As critical as I am about the Chinese model, one thing they seem to have mastered is stealing America's creations. From tobacco to pharmaceuticals to software, China's recklessness with intellectual property and patents is proof of its inherent lack of both contract laws and creative innovation.

Clearly most of China's manufacturing is properly licensed and legal. But even its legitimate industry mostly follows a cut-and-paste recipe, wherein it takes the products and processes of other economies and replicates them more cheaply using seemingly ever-abundant low-cost labor. Sometimes, it "takes"—as in steals without permission—as with Zippo. Most of the time it "takes"—meaning licensing and manufacturing legally and ethically—but nonetheless, only as a lower cost producer that adds little to no product value outside of cheaper labor. . . . And, it should be noted, when I say "takes," as in the case of Zippo, I literally mean without permission or licensing. The cut-and-paste process can, and surely has, produced incredible near-term income. It does not, however, present a model for sustainable, long-term growth. For example, China now produces more cars than any other country. But its contribution to auto design is negligible.

Long-term growth requires, above all else, innovation. First, because eventually the comparative advantage of cheap labor dissipates as wages rise, as is already occurring in China. And second, the ideas and products that truly create new wealth always emanate from great thinkers motivated by large profits, rather than by simply lowering production costs. So far, China has completely failed to move up the value-add design chain. And why? Are the Chinese not smart enough? Of course they are, but the economy and, indeed, the whole society suffocate under the repression of intolerance, central command, and censorship.

The danger of a lack of innovation is evident when we compare salaries of unskilled workers to those of university graduates. In 1998, China announced plans to bolster college attendance. Consequently, the annual number of graduates rose from about 800,000 per year to almost 6 million. But, in contrast to unskilled factory workers who easily find jobs in the East, these legions of university graduates struggle to find work. The *New York Times* has observed:

The supply of those trained in accounting, finance and computer programming now seems limitless, and their value has plunged. Between 2003 and 2009, the average starting salary for migrant laborers grew by nearly 80 percent; during the same period, starting pay for college graduates stayed the same, although their wages actually decreased if inflation is taken into account.[32]

These young workers struggle, and the educated classes perversely see relative wages declining—the exact opposite phenomenon evident in the United States. In China, the more educated the worker, the more depressing the opportunities, because China as a nation has failed to progress to higher-value businesses, a bitter outcome of a void of innovation. In China, stories of wealthy, well-connected contractors using Party-issued permits to build new high-rises abound. And loyal provincial officials share in the spoils of dreary textile mills producing basic products for the West at low cost. But very much lacking, despite 30 years of growth, are analogs to the Hewlett-Packard garage, where David Packard and Bill Hewlett launched their eponymous firm and spawned the entire Silicon Valley boom.

China has failed to so advance because its political and societal constraints on innovation preclude a true flowering of ideas and creativity. Watching the creative destruction of capitalism is not always pretty, and in fact is sometimes downright painful to those afflicted by change. But the inevitable and undeniable truth remains: Creation and destruction work wonders. Societies grow rich by allowing outliers to solve problems and create whole new businesses.

Moreover, the lack of transparency and void of innovation encourage all manner of inefficiencies. For example, China is already the world's second largest energy user, nearly matching the total energy consumed by the United States. But since its GDP is so much smaller, its energy used per unit of GDP ratio is only about one-third of the

U.S. level. And why? Mainly because state-owned enterprises pay little, or even nothing, for electricity. Are you a bit more willing to let the hot water run on and on in the shower of a hotel room or club locker room? Probably yes. On a much larger scale, the politically connected managers of Chinese factories often see little reason to conserve energy. In fact, they're so willing to "let the hot shower run" on China's cement producers, for example, that they use 45 percent more electricity per ton of output than comparable production elsewhere.[33]

Simply put, China is not a driving force of creative innovation. And without innovation, its growth prospects diminish greatly as its society ages and it loses the easy comparative advantage of endless free labor. But really, this void of innovation is not surprising. Rather, it directly flows from the folly of managing a country of 1.3 billion people with a small, secretive collection of allegedly omniscient overlords. As the great Austrian economist Friedrich Hayek remarked:

If the human intellect is allowed to impose a preconceived pattern on society, if our powers of reasoning are allowed to lay claim to a monopoly of creative effort . . . then we must not be surprised if society, as such, ceases to function as a creative force.[34]

Lasting growth requires innovation. Innovation requires openness. But China rejects these principles and will eventually reap the bitter harvest of a misguided and insular model. As we will examine in the concluding chapter of this book, America represents the near polar opposite of all these trends that so afflict China.

If China Catches a Cold, Who Else Will Start Sneezing?

First, it's important to note that, although the media and Wall Street research communities remain uniformly ebullient on China, actual capital might already be recognizing some of the risks I am detailing. For example, in 2010, a red-hot year for global equities in general, the S&P 500 Index climbed 13 percent and the German DAX rose 15 percent, but China's Shanghai Composite actually *declined* 14 percent. China's Shanghai markets are largely closed to foreigners, though, and are very volatile. Nevertheless, Chinese investors appear to be less willing to eat their own cooking than Western observers are. Even looking at the FXI I-Shares ETF, which trades in the United States and largely replicates the Hong Kong stock market (in U.S. dollar terms), from the beginning of 2010 through the first quarter 2011, FXI returned 7 percent gains versus the S&P's 19 percent gain over those same last five quarters.

Outside of China, the pain should be particularly acute for Australia, which has enjoyed a bit of a miracle growth cycle of its own recently, courtesy of China. Australia functions largely as "China's quarry" by sourcing the iron ore and copper necessary for the massive industrial projects of China. Largely due to exports to China, Australia has thrived in recent years even as the rest of the world peered over the edge during the 2008 credit crisis. In fact, as American housing craters with seemingly no bottom (see Chapter 4), Australia's property markets remain red-hot and its currency trades, as of March 2011, at a fresh 29-year high. But even a modest slowdown in China could quickly imperil the Australian expansion. That expansion Down Under appears very vulnerable, with Florida and Nevada 2007 types of real estate speculation. A study by *The Economist* recently found the Australian housing market almost 60 percent overvalued, the highest on earth (just above Hong Kong) based on price to income ratios and compared to similar rental rates.[35]

As such, I advise avoiding companies with too much Australian exposure, such as BHP Billiton. And for the more speculative and strong-stomached, shorting the Australian dollar via futures, spot FX markets, or the ETF EWA may pay handsomely.

Here in the United States, look to avoid or short the most China-centered companies, names like Caterpillar, General Motors, Union

Pacific Railroad, and United Technologies. But perhaps the simplest and safest way to play a China bubble bursting is to own U.S. Treasuries. A 2 percent yield on 10-year notes might not seem very appealing, but a volatile breakdown in China would send the world into further deflationary pressures. Since the collapse of Lehman Brothers and the credit crisis, the Federal Reserve has rightly been fearful of stubborn disinflationary, if not deflationary, pressures on the economy. As housing prices fall and wages stagnate, structural lower prices beckon. If China, with its massive existing overcapacity, starts to tank under a mountain of bad internal debt, then its only last-ditch hope will be to flood the world with cheap goods, even far below production cost. Such a scenario is frighteningly deflationary. And in that scenario, the world would run to the relative safety of the U.S. Treasury market.

While on the topic of Treasuries, it is worth mentioning that the media, like so many things China-related, completely misunderstand the dynamics of the United States-China debtor-creditor relationship. Yes, China owns a massive amount of Treasuries. And yes, the American government debt problem could spiral out of control if budget changes are not enacted. But who really has the bigger problem, America or China? The notion that China could sell Treasuries wholesale is absurd, as they would immediately realize massive losses for themselves by moving such a giant position quickly. No, the truth is that the Chinese have the problem regarding Treasuries. They are astutely concerned about the debt addiction of the federal government. But since a giant borrower always actually calls the shots to the creditor, it is simply the perverse reality of large-scale indebtedness. To put the situation in everyday terms, if you owe me $100, then it is your problem. If you owe me $1 million, then it is my problem. And the reality is that the Chinese have no alternative deployment for the massive amounts of cash flow they are presently generating from the United States. European sovereign issues weigh heavily on any Euro currency denominated bonds, and Japan's debt woes make the American situation seem downright frugal (as we will discuss in coming pages).

But America will hardly escape unscathed. Quite the opposite, in fact, given how much the developed world, America and Europe, have bet on China as the herd has rushed headlong into the Middle Kingdom. Far too many Americans have been seduced by the stunning scale and near-term efficiencies of economic dictatorship. Indeed, America's large companies, and billions of dollars of investment capital, have bet massively on China, believing the hype generated not just by Beijing but also by Wall Street and the media.

No matter how badly the West wants China to "thread the needle," the Chinese miracle will be revealed as merely a mirage. Central planning failed in the Soviet Union and it failed in Japan. Nor will it succeed in China. And when it unravels, Beijing will turn ever harder, like Michael Corleone, toward force and coercion. Because, like Corleone, the endgame for Beijing and the Party is not capital, but rather power. For now, capital suits the power calculus of the Party and so it dutifully pursues a quasi-capitalist policy of export industry. Once the breakneck pace of growth slows, the government will revert to its more Maoist tendencies toward insularity. Indeed, as Jim Chanos predicts: "Adam Smith is going to get his revenge in China."

Chapter 2

Dolls Are Meant for Children

Japan Stares into the Abyss of a Death Spiral

Japan has become, in our lifetimes, not the land of the rising sun, but the land of an extended, unceasing, colorless sun*set*; a march toward demographic implosion that will render its economy bankrupt and its geopolitical standing irrelevant. In P.D. James's book *The Children of Men*, an apocalyptic society can no longer reproduce children and the sterile would-be mothers tote baby dolls to maintain maternal sentiments in lieu of real infants. As dreary and convoluted as it may seem to us, this tale is not entirely far-fetched, not merely a fanciful projection, but in fact hints at the present and projected demographic realities of twenty-first century Japan.

As Mark Steyn explains in his macro-demographic tome, *America Alone: The End of the World As We Know It* (Regnery Publishing, 2008), in 2005 the Japanese toymaker Tomy, producer of the hit Transformer robots, began making a doll named Yumel, a baby designed as a companion to the elderly, serving as a fake grandchild for the massively growing legions of lonely, geriatric, grandchildless Japanese. A Tomy spokeswoman explains that "You can speak to the doll and she will tell you she loves you so much. If you hold the doll, the weight is the same weight as a small infant."[1] And this wonderbaby Yumel boasts a sort of bizarre older sibling named the Snuggling Ifbot, whose purpose is to converse with the elderly using the phrases of a five-year-old child, in part to prevent senility. In present-day Japan, at least, dolls are clearly not just for children. Instead, the childless, or at least grandchildless, oldsters of Japan would like to act like children, holding dolls instead of humans. As Steyn explains in *America Alone*, they themselves are "the children they never had." In time, perhaps a new industry will arise, manufacturing high-end baby-jogger strollers for the fake children so that elderly Japanese can visit the Osaka Zoo and leisurely stroll with their fake little Yumels, enjoying the sights.

Similarly, in a country witnessing plummeting birthrates, the business of childbirth becomes unattractive as a no-growth industry. Hence, Japan is witnessing a dearth of obstetricians. On Oki Island, a town of 17,000 people, the obstetrician arrives like clockwork every Monday and stays from 10 A.M. until 5:30 P.M. The Japanese are rightly known as a precise and punctual people, but even the Japanese of Oki might have trouble hitting the "birth bull's-eye" of a Monday luncheon birth.

The Yumel doll and the dearth of obstetricians give anecdotal evidence to the macro reality that women in Japan have simply taken themselves out of the business of giving birth. Their mothers may have dutifully endured living with the 1970s Japanese "salary man" husband who worked 85 hours a week and drank a good portion of the remaining waking hours with his work colleagues, but contemporary young Japanese woman are loudly proclaiming "no thanks." In fact, the majority of Japanese women born in the 1970s, all of whom are 30 years and older now, have not yet birthed even one child. Moreover, the average Japanese child today has a completely vertical family tree. That is, they have parents and grandparents, but no siblings, no aunts and uncles, and no cousins. An anecdotal proof of this lonely Japanese recession in people was noted by my friend and noted market maven Dennis Gartman, of *The Gartman Letter*, who points out that "Japan sells more adult diapers than baby diapers."[2]

This lack of reproduction ensures that Japan, an island nation becoming increasingly a financial island of debt-related recklessness, will be the first among industrial nations to face the crushing impact of runaway indebtedness, and eventually will become an almost forgotten, insignificant Pacific island rather than the global economic powerhouse of just a quarter-century ago.

The idea of grandparents cuddling fake children instead of real children represents a sad societal failure. But the point of this book is not sociology, but economics and profit. And in this chapter, we will examine how the severe demographic and fiscal implosion of Japan will force a financial market reckoning far worse than the previous two lost decades of no growth in Japan. Admittedly, unlike China, Japan's problems are well advertised, and much more widely believed. So, on first blush, it might appear that I am not presenting quite as contrarian an idea. But on closer examination, I am indeed presenting a contrarian, maverick "against the herd" idea regarding Japan because I am arguing that Japan's problems are utterly terminal, that there is literally no escape from the death spiral. I also submit that recent events are hastening the demise of Japan, and therefore the time for investment mavericks to start betting against Japan is right now.

We're Number Two (clap) . . .
We're Number Two (clap) . . .

America has never, relative to the rest of the world, held a more powerful position economically, militarily, and politically as today. In the concluding chapter of this book I will detail the many structural and cultural advantages that will ensure not only a continuation of this leadership, but in fact a marked acceleration of America's hegemony. But almost as remarkable as America's actual standing is its continual negative, self-indicting, doubtful *perception* of its standing.

Americans, and especially American elites, seem to perpetually seek to emulate the alleged new number-one rival to America. During much of the Cold War, that rival was the Soviet Union. The USSR's central planning, and accomplishments in science, and even sports, seemed to signal a model superior to America's decentralized individualism. As I detailed in Chapter 1, more recently Americans of all stripes, but especially the intelligentsia elites, join almost uniformly in the opinion that China will rise and eclipse American power on every front. In the 1980s, the American "we're number two" thematic melody progressed to a distinctively Japanese beat, as predictions of Japanese supremacy dominated business, academia, Main Street, entertainment, and financial markets.

In 1986, Ron Howard directed the hit film *Gung Ho*, starring Michael Keaton as an American official in an American plant purchased by the Japanese. The movie highlighted the dominant economic stereotypes of the 1980s: the Japanese as brilliant, aggressive, hardworking automatons in contrast to the Americans as lazy, bloated, selfish underlings. Along the same lines, the 1989 hit *Die Hard*, with Bruce Willis, took place in the fictional Nakatomi Plaza in Los Angeles. Although the plot really had little to do with the Japanese, the subtext was nonetheless clear to both Willis's John McClane character and to the American audience: You Americans work for us now. In reality, the movie set for Nakatomi Plaza was the very American-owned Fox Plaza, in which President Ronald Reagan occupied the penthouse as his post-White House Presidential office. As an adolescent in the 1980s, I vividly recall seeing all the cool kids donning Rising Sun T-shirts and headbands as all things Japanese came into vogue. And of course, like the present-day rush we mentioned in Chapter 1 to "teach little Junior to speak Mandarin," in the 1980s the language was Japanese.

Outside of pop culture, more intellectual realms were similarly effusive in praising Japan. Perhaps the foundational intellectual underpinning of this theme was the 1980 work *Japan As Number One*, by Harvard professor Ezra Vogel (Harvard University Press). Speaking of number one, this book in fact reached the number-one spot on the Japanese bestseller list and earned widespread acclaim in the United States. Another voice from the academy, Dean Meredith Woo of the University of Virginia, explained that "Japan seemed superior to America in every way."[3] Dr. Lester Thurow, the dean of the Sloan School of Business at Massachusetts Institute of Technology, became a rarity among business school professors—a pop culture figure. He regularly and viciously vilified not just President Reagan and his free market policies, but in fact the whole notion of American capitalism. Conversely, he elevated Japanese methods as unbeatable paths to enduring prosperity, earning himself accolades on the TV show *60 Minutes*, and he wrote an acclaimed book, *Head to Head: The Coming Economic Battle Among Japan, Europe and America*, in which he claimed that "If one looks at the last 20 years, Japan would have to be considered the betting favorite to win the economic honors of owning the 21st century."[4]

But was Japan, in fact, superior? Or was it an unsustainable mirage, and indeed a prequel, as it were, to the China story of today? I argue for the latter explanation, that Japan's 1980s surge, while incredibly impressive, was, at its foundation, unsustainable, and that its present decline will soon accelerate. This afflicts the average investor with unrecognized risk, and presents the maverick investor with untold opportunity.

A Whole New World?

It's difficult now to recall, in that period a quarter of a century ago, just how dominant the Japanese appeared economically. Like Aladdin in the Disney rendition of the fable, it appeared that the Japanese showed the rest of us "A Whole New World." The country had risen, phoenix-like, from the ashes of World War II. Demoralized and occupied, the country bravely rebuilt, inspired by the leadership of General

Douglas MacArthur and funded by the generosity of the American taxpayer. In fact, Japan successfully moved up the value-added chain of production impressively (in stark contrast, incidentally, to present-day China, which remains mired in low-innovation production). Japan first fully exploited its comparative labor cost advantage, and throughout the 1950s and 1960s became a key low-cost supplier of rudimentary American consumer goods. Into the 1970s, though, Japan embarked on a focused campaign of government-led industrial policy. Tokyo's leadership determined that Japan would dominate selected industries, especially automobiles, consumer electronics, and steel, and take market share from an America beset by inflation, tepid capital markets, and staggeringly high interest rates. Japan's government, in fact, operated the quasi-private banking system as a de facto arm of the Japanese state, mandating credit and interest rate policies from on high.

At first, this policy of loose capital, meaning plenty of lending and credit for industrial companies and mandated low interest rates, worked well. Traditional savers anyway, the Japanese willingly plowed earnings from the impressive post-World War II recovery into the coffers of Japanese banks, accepting artificially low rates and creating a banking system flush with cash. But while Japanese banks boasted massive capital reserves into the 1980s, what they lacked was prudence in lending. At the behest of the lauded industrial policy of Japan, an intertwined system of banking-to-industrial cross-ownership and indebtedness abounded. Sumitomo Bank loaned money to Sumitomo Industries, which then bought shares in the bank, which in turn lent more money to the industrial firm, and so on. The Japanese proved that creating cash flow is relatively easy. A centrally planned, top-down command economy can easily exploit a mercantilist approach and export mightily, given artificially low interest rates. But the eventual hangover from such a credit bender is not pleasant. And in Japan's case, the hangover is, in fact, leading to a terminal illness. What such an expansion of credit does not produce is profits, at least not in any lasting sense.

While the boom persisted, the results were admittedly most impressive. Japanese shares rallied hard throughout almost all the 1980s and price-to-earnings ratios of 100 were commonplace. Market analysts and financial media lauded the inherent superiority of the Japanese model and superiority of the collectivist, all-together-now, Japanese culture. In fact, by the late 1980s, the market capitalization, or total value, of Japanese stocks exceeded that of the United States, even though the American economy was twice as large at the time. So exuberantly did global capital embrace the Japanese that the market capitalization of just one company, Nippon Telegraph and Telephone (NTT), exceeded the value of the entire German stock market.[5] To gauge just how far Japanese valuations have already descended, NTT's market capitalization today stands at $58 billion. An impressive and large company, to be sure, but not even close to being as large as one German company, SAP, which is a software rival to Oracle. (SAP, incidentally, while larger than NTT, for reference purposes is less than half as large as Oracle, meaning that a company that once exceeded the total value of all Germany is now less than one-third the value of just one successful American firm).

In 2011 the inherent danger in Japanese shares may seem obvious, but at the late 1980s high only the most contrarian maverick thinkers doubted the Japanese model. In fact, at the height of the Nikkei, fully eight of the largest ten companies in the world, by market capitalization, were Japanese. Presently, not one of the top ten is Japanese. Regarding GDP, in 1990 Japan represented 14 percent of the global economy, and today it represents a paltry—and quickly diminishing—8 percent.[6] The shares bubble ended on the last day of trading in 1989, when the Nikkei closed at 38,916. Since then it has declined over 80 percent to its 2009 low of 7,055 and has done little since (see Figure 2.1). In 1990 alone, the Nikkei fell almost 40 percent, and declined 60 percent from its peak within two years, a stunning reversal for an economy that appeared unapproachable just months earlier. Maverick thinking can, at least, prevent following the herd of cattle off a cliff such as the Nikkei of the late 1980s. And at its best, maverick investing can actually reap significant profit from recognizing when the herd is vulnerable, as was certainly the case with Japan in the late 1980s. Later in this chapter, I

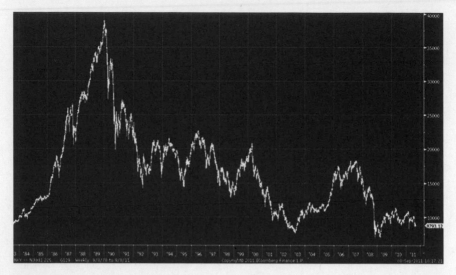

Figure 2.1   Nikkei 225 Index, 1988 to July 2011

will detail what I envision as the brutal conclusion to the Japan drama, and how we can all protect and grow capital in that scenario.

But first, we should examine how a bubble in the proportions of the Japanese equity bubble could form. What factors propelled capital to so believe in this chimera? And where, other than the Nikkei, did this thinking also infect and instill pain?

Brother, Can You Spare a Yen?

In 1985 the central bankers and finance ministers of the world's largest countries determined in concert that the super-strong United States dollar needed to depreciate. After that agreement, the yen strengthened dramatically. At that time, the United States government was borrowing at then-record peacetime levels, mostly to fund the mammoth Reagan military expansion and fight the Cold War. The owners of that ballooning debt were largely the Japanese. As the U.S. dollar cheapened against their yen, the real value of their U.S. Treasury holdings began to erode. Consequently the Japanese began repatriating capital, selling American assets, and bringing the capital back to Japan, which only served to spur a further yen rally.

But the Bank of Japan feared this strengthening yen as an impediment to the key (and largely government-controlled) export companies. So the Bank of Japan fought the yen appreciation through lower interest rates, bringing the discount lending rate down to just 2.5 percent by 1987, the lowest point since World War II. With an inflation rate higher than that 2.5 percent, the Bank of Japan was, quite literally, giving away money, pumping massive liquidity into their financial system. As George Friedman stated in his book, *The Next 100 Years: A Forecast for the 21st Century*, "Certainly Japan was growing rapidly, but its rapid growth had less to do with management than with Japan's banking system."[7] Super-low rates combined with a strong yen created the tinder for a classic bonfire of reckless investment.

They Own Pebble Beach *and* Rockefeller Center?

And invest they did. The Japanese went on a global shopping spree in the late 1980s that might embarrass the profligate *Housewives of Orange County*. Speaking of California, they bought famed Pebble Beach golf course. Imagine if, in the 1950s, you played a round at Pebble Beach with Bing Crosby and told him that Japan, the just-defeated, demoralized enemy of America, would someday own his favorite links? If there is one certainty in predicting future political and economic trends, it is to expect conventional wisdom to be wrong. Although the Japanese were bidding up real estate globally, including buying Rockefeller Center in New York, they were even more aggressive at home regarding property. At the height, the land value of the imperial palace in Tokyo exceeded the total land value of, not just Pebble Beach, but in fact the entire state of California.[8]

Such a bubble was bound to pop, and it did with fierce power. As poorly as American property markets have traded in recent years, our problems pale compared to the massive pain inflicted on Japan in the early 1990s. Values of commercial real estate in Japan receded a whopping 87 percent.[9] Combined with the Nikkei free-fall that had commenced in 1990 as well, Japan saw its national wealth erode with stunning rapidity. As a result, there has been no job growth and no nominal GDP growth since. Young adults studying today in Japanese universities have *never* lived in a growing, prosperous economy.

Regarding those investments in marquee American properties, the eventual loss to Japanese mogul Minoru Isutani was a total of $340 million on the golf course. American billionaire Marvin Davis now looked like a genius for selling it to the Japanese. And Rockefeller Center was an epic disaster. Mitsubishi Estate Company ended up literally turning over the keys to the trust that held the mortgage, realizing a walloping $1 billion loss.

By 1993, the Japanese government finally realized, far too late, that Japan's bubble was badly burst, and tried to fight with lower interest rates. But it was already too late since dangerous deflation had set in, meaning a complete lack of pricing power in the economy as all consumers demanded lower prices to spend on anything, from real estate to clothing. In the first quarter of 1993, overall prices declined by 1.1 percent. By mid-1993, prices were falling at a Great Depression-like 4.2 percent.[10]

The "Portfolio" Account

When I started working as a bright-eyed Treasury broker in the early 1990s, the Japanese, while clearly in macro decline, were still massive players in American capital markets and especially in the U.S. Treasury markets. My bosses covered a wide range of Japanese accounts, both in Tokyo and in the American branches of Japanese banks. Though less than two decades removed, I am amazed today at the complete void of obvious Japanese participation in our capital markets. But back then, even as the Nikkei and Japanese real estate rolled over, the Japanese were still major market movers in the capital markets of the West. I found the Japanese to be far more cavalier about risk than our institutional accounts in New York and Europe. This cowboy attitude from a mostly reserved group of people seemed odd.

One day, having beers with a young Japanese trader talking markets, I asked about a particularly large, losing Treasury position they'd executed through our desk. Had he offset the trade using other brokers, I asked, or hedged it in some other way? A bit emboldened perhaps from drinking the chemical courage at happy hour, he laughed loudly, shook his head "no," and slapped his knee. "That position, Steven-san, has been moved to our portfolio account." A losing position is a loser no matter what account it inhabits, so I did not grasp the relevance (or the humor) of the explanation. What the young trader meant, I learned, was that losing near-term trades could simply be allocated to longer term "portfolio" accounts, becoming no longer the problem of the trading desk or the trader, but instead a macro problem for the bank as a whole. It was analogous to a baseball pitcher loading the bases with no outs, and then leaving the game without any consequences. As I later discovered, this "portfolio" practice was widespread and contributed greatly to the demise of Japanese banks as global players in capital markets.

Indeed, this problem of adding banking risk as the crisis deepened was not limited to trading desks, but also applied to lending. Low rates had fueled all manner of risky lending, and now with prices plummeting, those businesses could not repay the debts. But instead of writing off these obligations, with government complicity the Japanese covered up many of these de facto defaults by lending even *more* money to troubled borrowers. American banks acted similarly recklessly in terms of lending in the 2005 to 2007 period. And, like Japan, those banks were encouraged by the credit boom that followed a period of government easy money policy, in the American case following September 11. But, in stark contrast to the Japanese, in the United States transparency has been the norm in dealing with these problems once the bubble bursts. Writedowns have been aggressive, and both business and government clearly acknowledge the severity and reality of the problem. Credit, especially in housing, is contracting rapidly, in opposition to the initial Japanese reaction. In Japan, akin to my trader client moving problem risk into the "portfolio" account, bank lenders kicking the can down the road by extending even more credit backfired. Giving a whiskey to the town drunk rarely works, and it did not for Japanese banking. Nor does real life work like the Henny Youngman joke: "The doctor told me I have six months to live. I told him I couldn't pay my bill, and he gave me another six months."

Neither a Borrower Nor a Lender Be

In Shakespeare's *Hamlet*, Polonius delivers a sort of avuncular recipe for success in life speech to his nephew Laertes, advising him on "best practices" as he journeys off to university to study, become a man, and find his way in the world. One of the most memorable lines is "neither a borrower nor a lender be." Polonius knew instinctively that debt can be meddlesome at best, crippling at worst, whether on the lending or borrowing side of the balance sheet. Too late now, but Japan should have translated Polonius's speech into Japanese and mailed a copy to every person on the island.

Japan faces, quite simply, a bond trap that is now inescapable, a terminal death spiral of debt that is just beginning to strangle the economy of Japan and ensure that it cannot recover for generations, if ever. Its debt-to-GDP ratios have reached nightmarish proportions. The total ratio now exceeds 200 percent, the highest in the developed world by far. And its debt-to-private GDP ratio stands at an even worse 240 percent. Incredibly, Japan now finds itself in the most untoward fiscal company of Zimbabwe, Sudan, and Egypt in the debt-to-GDP rankings (see Figure 2.2). It is hard to fathom how a country as advanced as Japan, with bullet trains and world-class medicine, could be lumped in fiscally with economic basket cases like Sudan, but the math does not lie.

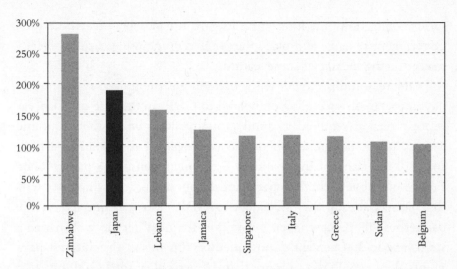

Figure 2.2 Debt-GDP with Japan and Third World Countries
SOURCE: John Mauldin, *Endgame* (Hoboken, NJ: John Wiley & Sons, 2011). Reprinted with permission of John Wiley & Sons, Inc.

Japan is not alone in this predicament; the entire world has embarked on an unprecedented debt binge. This borrowing mostly represents a grand attempt to forestall a most necessary process of rational global deleveraging that must occur. But Japan's predicament does stand alone as singularly severe, due to the scale of the borrowing and its demographics. I will examine the demographics in the following pages of this chapter, but first I will detail the precarious nature of the Japanese national indebtedness.

X's and O's

I coach high school football for fun and love the challenge of game planning, the chess match of X's and O's on a whiteboard (chalkboards are so passé!). A game I would not want to be game planning for, at the Bank of Japan and Ministry of Finance, is the arrival of X-day, as it is being called within trading circles. That day is when Japanese debt service obligations, the interest on its gargantuan debt, exceed the total government revenue and place the country into an inescapable checkmate, forcing default of some nature.

One reason this showdown is hastening is the trajectory of interest payments rapidly ascending compared to GDP. In the case of Japan, far more capital is required to fund growing debt, while the economic activity of the nation, and hence its tax revenue, is stagnating at best. In 2010 the Bank of International Settlements released a paper, "The Future of Public Debt: Prospects and Implications," in which it asserts that Japan's already excessive debt-to-GDP ratio will not stay at the dangerous 200 percent level, but within the next decade will soar to a stratospheric 300 percent. Consequently, this means that interest payments alone would rise to more than 10 percent of total GDP by 2025 for Japan. See Figure 2.3.

For the past 20 years, despite the skepticism of most capital market traders and analysts, Japan has been able to successfully finance its endless attempts at government stimuli because domestic companies, especially insurance firms, and individual Japanese savers have dutifully purchased an almost endless stream of JGBs—Japanese Government Bonds. But the famously thrifty Japanese are fast drawing down savings and the trajectory is certain and points toward an aging nation of net spenders, not savers. Japan began the two lost decades with a savings rate at 16 percent. It has slowly dipped to 2 percent and will soon likely head to negative territory. The realities of slow growth and a population bell curve moving ever-older is depleting the savings of the nation. Moreover, the Japanese government has, for years, relied heavily on somewhat abusive reliance on public pensions to buy JGBs. For example, the three largest holders of JGBs are the Japan Post Bank, the Government Pension Investment Fund, and Japan Post Insurance. But recent growth from these groups in JGB holdings is barely positive and likely headed to negative numbers, in line with macro levels of Japanese savings.

Without the Japanese individual saver and public Japanese funds to support this debt orgy, the Japanese will soon be compelled to seek credit in the international capital markets, as the United States presently

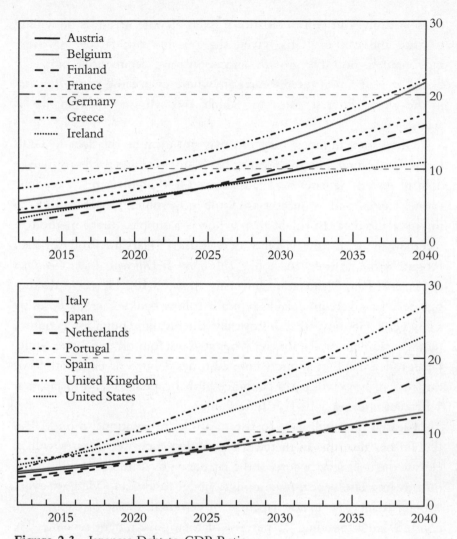

Figure 2.3 Japanese Debt-to-GDP Ratio

SOURCE: John Mauldin, *Endgame* (Hoboken, NJ: John Wiley & Sons, 2011). Reprinted with permission of John Wiley & Sons, Inc.

does so easily. But will international fixed income investors be willing to take the risk of JGBs, given the massive risk factors of over-indebtedness, no GDP growth, and population decimation? Not very likely, at least not at interest rates anywhere even close to the lowest-in-the-world interest rates to which the Ministry of Finance is accustomed.

The scariest numbers for Japan may not even be the debt-to-GDP ratios, foreboding though they may be. Many investors prefer to analyze debt to government revenue ratio, since GDP involves many complicating factors and is subject to some government machinations to improve the data. But debt to revenue is a simple, direct method to ascertain the cash flow viability of a country. Harvard Professor Ken Rogoff wrote an excellent book, *This Time Is Different: Eight Centuries of Financial Folly* (Princeton University Press, 2010). He correctly recognizes that sovereign defaults typically follow banking/credit crises by a few years. He shows that, historically, the breaking point for a country requiring foreign capital for credit tips at about four times debt/revenue. Japan today stands at an incredible 20 times debt to revenue ratio! For this reason, how will Japan convince global capital to lend to Japan at 1 percent rates on a 10-year time frame?

Clearly, rates will have to rise to attract international money. But therein lies the rub. Even the most modest increases in rates will so elevate the debt service costs of the Japanese government that Japan tips quickly into insolvency. According to hedge fund titan Kyle Bass, every 1 percent increase in the Japanese government's cost of capital will consume an astounding 25 percent of total government revenue. He states, "For context, if Japan had to borrow at France's rate, the interest burden alone would bankrupt the government."[11] In fact, I believe in all likelihood Japan would have to pay an interest rate higher than Germany, a country in far sounder fiscal condition, which currently pays about 2.0 percent for 10-year debt, more than double the interest rate of Japan.

So Japan is trapped. They are caught in a bond death spiral, having exhausted the savings of an aging nation. For 20 years, through an unceasing stream of ever-grander public stimuli, the government of Japan has acted like a spoiled trust fund adolescent, depending on a wealthy uncle to fund the party. But the uncle no longer earns and is aging apace. In reality, the Japanese debt situation resembles the Ponzi scheme of Madoff. Not to say that Japan is hiding anything—this whole Japan scenario is quite transparent. But it is Madoff-esque nonetheless in that once the flow of money from investors slows, the whole charade turns in on itself and implodes. Even Prime Minister Kan admitted as much in June 2010 when he stated, "If Japan fails to tackle fiscal reform, we could come under the control of bodies like the International Monetary Fund, which could tell us what to do in the sovereign matter of fiscal management."[12]

So what will become the endgame for Japan? When X-day arrives, Japan faces no alternative but a massive printing of the yen, which would be a large scale devaluation. The Bank of Japan will have to step in and buy the whole auction itself, creating yen out of thin air. At the end of this chapter, we will investigate ways to avoid risk and/or profit from this inevitable showdown, the most compelling of which is buying U.S. dollars and selling yen. But first, we need to dig into the demographic realities of Japan.

Austin Powers Would Not Enjoy Japan

In this world, only a few certainties exist. We will eventually die. The Chicago Cubs will never win a World Series. Teenage boys are lust crazed . . . unless they happen to be Japanese. Quite incredibly, the London Telegraph reports that in 2010 fully 35 percent of Japanese males aged 16 through 19 report they have no interest in sex, a doubling from the 2008 survey. Dr Kunio Kitamura of the Japanese Family Planning Association reports that "the most important reason for Japan's declining birthrate is that people are not having sex."[13]

The average American 19-year-old male could probably stand to focus a bit less on the carnal. But given a choice between a country that is too sexual and one where teenage boys have become (mentally, at least) uninterested in it, my investing preference will skew toward the country that is on the more aggressive side. America's per-woman birthrate remains at replacement 2.1, whereas Japan transposes that figure into 1.2 births per woman. Add in America's global status as immigration destination for the world, and the future promises growth for America and retrenchment for Japan.

Regardless of what fixates the Japanese young man, most Japanese women have simply removed themselves from the birthing business. The problem with demographics is that the math works inversely even faster than when the population is growing. For example, in 1989, 11.5 percent of Japan was over 65 years old. Projections then indicated that the country would be 25 percent over 65 by 2030. In fact, here in 2011, Japan has already almost reached that mark, two full decades early. Stagnant incomes and prudish young men can have that effect. And immigration appears to be a totally culturally unacceptable alternative. Japan has never believed in assimilation of outsiders. For example, in 2007, the United Nations High Commission of Refugees reports that the United States accepted 50,000 refugees—Japan took in 41. So, in reality, Austin Powers faces two reasons to avoid Japan: its lack of virility and its distrust of outsiders. Because of this dearth of immigration and low birth rate, Japan's total population will be halved within 50 years (see Figure 2.4).

2011 Natural Disaster

On March 11, 2011, Japan was struck with the most powerful earthquake in its history, and one of the five most powerful worldwide since modern record keeping began in 1900. This earthquake spawned a tsunami (a word invented by the Japanese, roughly meaning "harbor wave") that devastated the northeast coast of Japan. In total, well over 10,000 lives were lost, 125,000 buildings destroyed, and a nuclear plant rendered useless and potentially dangerous for years to come. The financial fallout is estimated by the Japanese government to exceed

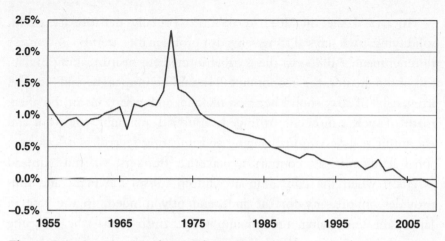

Figure 2.4 Japanese Population Change Since 1955
SOURCE: A. Gary Shilling, *The Age of Deleveraging* (Hoboken, NJ: John Wiley & Sons, 2010).
Reprinted with permission of John Wiley & Sons, Inc.

$300 billion, making this earthquake the world's most expensive disaster ever.

Incredibly, consensus among media and investment analysts has focused on the supposedly net positive stimulative impact of the disaster upon the Japanese economy. For example, chief global economist of Nomura securities Paul Sheard wrote: "This is exactly what deflation-ridden Japan needs. Japan's GDP deflator has fallen by 15% since its peak in the second quarter of 1994, while the US GDP deflator is up 40% in that period."[14] Many bulls on Japan point to the severe 1995 Kobe earthquake and its aftermath. The Japanese economy did indeed witness a strong, albeit brief, renaissance following the Kobe quake, and perhaps directly related to the Kobe rebuild. But, in 1995, Japan was still a major global economic power and its fiscal condition, while deteriorating, was nowhere near as perilous as it stands in 2011. Moreover, the era of no-growth had just begun—economically and in population—and so the all-important psychology of deflation, thrift, and recession has not yet become branded onto Japanese minds.

In fact, I see the 2011 quake as a brutally deflationary event, solidifying and crystallizing already problematic trends in Japan's retrenchment. Adding to the terrible immediate heartbreaking human toll of the disaster, the economic toll should be immediate and, frankly, irreversible. I may sound heartless making such assertions in the aftermath of such a momentous tragedy. But if I am right, the fiscal and economic realities are unchanging and uncaring regardless of our personal sentiments. As contrarian, maverick thinkers, we must instead ascertain when the conventional wisdom misses the mark and thus provides opportunity for the independently minded. In the case of Japan, the underlying, though unpopular, truth is that the endgame process is quickening, largely because of the earthquake/tsunami.

First, the disaster puts enormous pressure on already depressed prices. When struck with tragedy of any kind, people naturally—and correctly—retrench to safety. The Japanese are already accustomed to ever-lower prices. They therefore spend reluctantly, and demand small profit margins of the producers of whatever product is being purchased. Witnessing the destruction of a sizable piece of their nation, this instinct will only accelerate. Moreover, and more important, in a country that is not growing, in people or in GDP, the incentive to rebuild aggressively simply does not exist. For example, would a warehouse owner in Sedai whose plant was destroyed, when analyzing years of declining profits in a town of fast-declining population, rebuild at or near the same scale as before the tsunami? We find it unlikely, as long as he is a remotely rational actor. For this reason, the 2011 Japan disaster differs dramatically from similar events elsewhere, and even previously in Japan itself. For example, when San Francisco was struck in 1907 with a devastating earthquake, the city rebuilt bigger and more efficiently than before the quake. Similarly, Chicago resurged at a breakneck pace from its 1871 devastating fire. But both of those cities were thriving and growing rapidly before the disasters. Companies and individuals, therefore, had the confidence to quickly rebuild, and in fact expand, seeing the ruins as an opportunity. In the case of Japan, sadly, the ruins will be seen as an exaggerated reminder of the already diminishing opportunities in twenty-first century Japan.

In addition, the massive public borrowing and spending necessary to pay for the mammoth damages inflicted will, in fact, bring X-day ever closer. In the aftermath of the disaster, the Bank of Japan quickly doubled its asset purchase program to 10 trillion yen, trying desperately to increase liquidity to the shocked economy. In addition to this monetary action, on the fiscal side Japan is set to raise taxes to help pay for the swelling government budget in reaction to the disaster. In a strong economy, a credible argument could be made that these stimulative measures would spur growth and help recovery. But in insanely debt-burdened Japan, such measures will instead add gasoline to an already dangerous fire of impending insolvency.

The X Factor: How to Invest as Japan Declines

All of these failures of central planning, combined with the macro barriers of debt and demography, are now fusing with the tragedy of the March natural disasters to propel Japan on a permanent path toward bankruptcy and, ultimately, global irrelevancy. It is almost hard to exaggerate how far our economic esteem for Japan has fallen, from feared global business hegemony of the 1980s to the G-10 poster child for bad policy just over two decades later. Perhaps an equally unpopular, but just as certain, future reality will be a Japan that stops slowly, deliberately shrinking, and instead starts to economically implode.

What will be the methods for the maverick investor to avoid peril and capture profit in this scenario? First, avoiding or shorting Japanese equities makes sense. The successful manager of British hedge fund Eclectica, Hugh Hendry, is enacting a strategy that straddles the Japan-China trade relationship. He made a name for himself successfully betting against Greek debt in 2010. Now he points out how heavily exposed Japan's banks are to China. Those banks have been aggressively selling credit default swaps (credit insurance protection) on Japanese firms such as Nippon Steel that have benefited hugely from the China building boom. Hendry is, therefore, buying such CDS products. Any combination of China/Japan downturns should seriously increase the value of such insurance. Hendry may well be onto something, as Japanese Banks in 2010 sank to their lowest level since 1983, as recorded by the Topix Banks Index. Further, that index has trailed the MSCI World Bank Index since mid 2009.[15] As for the exposure of American companies, they have invested far less in Japan than they have in China. So the China crash scenario remains the central risk for American multinationals that have not exported much to the frugal Japanese consumer.

Shorting Japanese companies themselves presents one plausible way to profit from the coming implosion of Japan. Toyota and Sony, for example, trade as ADRs (American Depositary Receipts) on the New York Stock Exchange. But the problem is that, as the yen weakens dramatically, those kinds of transactions will gain serious currency advantages in exporting globally. So even though their domestic markets will shrink greatly, international demand could partially offset those losses, and shorting Nikkei or its components may not be the best method of exposure.

Instead, the simplest method is shorting the Japanese currency itself and buying the U.S. dollar. First because, as we have discussed, the only solution for X-day is a wholesale devaluation of the currency, wherein the Bank of Japan steps up and supports the entire JGB auction by buying the Japanese debt with money it simply creates by fiat with a wave of a monetary wand. And second, because this implosion in Japan will ultimately create massive deflationary pressure on the world, which should elevate the status and value of the American dollar. Though rapidly receding, Japan still represents a major portion of the world economy. Removing much of that demand, and exporting cheaper goods globally through a depreciating yen, will force global prices lower. In these scenarios, the much maligned U.S. dollar wins.

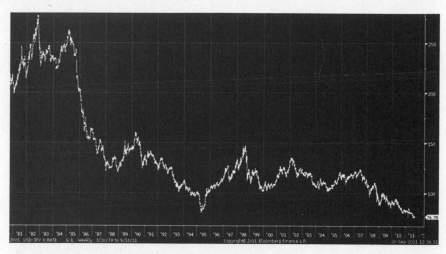

Figure 2.5 Japanese Yen per U.S. Dollar since 1980
SOURCE: Bloomberg LLP.

Again, only individual thinkers today can buck the trend of pervasive dollar negativity and ascertain the inherent relative advantages of the American economy and currency.

For all of the 1980s, the USD/JPY dollar/yen currency pair traded above 120 yen per dollar, and it spent a good part of that decade above 200. See Figure 2.5. In recent times following the 2011 disaster, USD/ JPY traded all the way down to 76 yen per dollar. In our money printing default projection, we see USD/JPY trading, again, well above 100, and perhaps even testing the 200 levels not seen in 25 years. For investors unable to trade the currencies themselves, in either spot markets or futures, the FXY ETF is fairly liquid and trades as a proxy for the foreign exchange pair. Bearish bets on the yen mean buying USD/JPY in currency markets, and shorting FXY in the ETF realm. If shorting Japanese shares, I would focus on those more domestically oriented, who might not gain as much export advantage from a currency devaluation. But one domestic firm I would not short is Tomy, because I think they are really onto something with that Yumel doll being cuddled by the growing masses of grandchildless Japanese oldsters.

Chapter 3

Can't Touch This

Resist the Allure of Gold

In 1990 a singer named Stanley Kirk Burrell, far better known as MC Hammer, rushed onto the rap scene with his breakout single, "Can't Touch This." At that time, gold traded for about $400 an ounce. Fast-forward two decades to MC Hammer starring in a Super Bowl commercial for Cash4Gold, a Pompano Beach, Florida, gold refinery company in which Hammer took an equity stake, agreeing to become its celebrity sponsor. He appeared alongside now-deceased Ed McMahon, of *Tonight Show with Johnny Carson* fame. Both celebrities were bouncing back financially after losing large fortunes, and they declared that the path to riches is paved with none other than the yellow metal—gold.

I do not share MC Hammer's enthusiasm for the yellow metal. In fact, the recent surge in gold and silver presents yet another dangerous market bubble that will surely end in tears and the gnashing of teeth. Admittedly, I am indeed arguing against a tidal wave of human lust for gold. Going back a bit further in history before Hammer, in 1519 my supposed ancestor, Hernán Cortés (family lineage is unclear, though my father claimed to be a descendant) famously declared to Montezuma, the ruler of the Aztecs, that "We Spaniards suffer from a disease that only gold can cure." In seeking their cure, Cortés and his army commenced a conquest that would eliminate Aztec rule and eventually claim all of Latin America as possessions of Spain, and also expropriate vast sums of gold for themselves and the Spanish crown. A few years later, fellow conquistador Francisco Pizarro displayed a level of greed for the yellow metal that might have embarrassed even Hernán. As ransom to release the Inca king of Peru, Pizarro successfully demanded a "ransom room" filled entirely with gold, measuring 22 × 17 feet, and reaching above the poor King Atahualpa's head.

The Spaniards, however, had more legitimate rationales for gold lust than the conspiratorial gold bugs of today. In the Renaissance era, gold was a highly transportable store of wealth, in an age of primitive banking and undependable currencies. Moreover, in that pre-industrial era, other more usable commodities held little value.

But today's lust for gold makes little sense, and in fact presents a dangerous greater-fool scheme, in which every believer stands utterly dependent upon convincing another investor to buy into an anachronistic, useless, and almost unanalyzable asset. The maverick investor, always keenly aware of the temporary madness of the masses, will avoid jumping on the tempting, but illogical, precious metals bandwagon. For aggressive investors/traders, betting against the precious metals mania may present untold opportunities for profit. In fact, the unwind in gold may well present opportunities for profit resembling the collapse of the housing bubble, ably exploited by independent thinkers like Dr. Michael Burry, whom I profiled in the introduction.

In this chapter, I lay out the case *against* gold. Contrary to popular opinion, inflationary fears are overblown; printing by the federal government is not creating a velocity of money; gold is a poor inflation hedge anyway; and the bullish gold trade is far too crowded for comfort.

How Deep Is Your Love?

In 1977 John Travolta electrified moviegoers with his performance in the movie *Saturday Night Fever*, spreading the disco culture globally and popularizing Bee Gees' hits like "How Deep Is Your Love." The lead character, Tony Manero, worked a dead-end job at a neighborhood Brooklyn hardware store. Despite his meager earnings, Tony could easily afford the gold chains he preferred, since gold then traded for just above $100 an ounce. But within a few years, a massive precious metals rally would occur—sending gold to $850 an ounce in 1980—before promptly melting back down to earth. The same time period saw an even more massive bubble in silver. The Hunt brothers, Texas oil heir billionaires, tried unsuccessfully to corner the market on silver, sending its price from $6 an ounce up to almost $50 an ounce. Once the Hunts were forced out of their massive and highly leveraged position, they lost over $1 billion on the scheme and sent silver prices back down into the low teens.

As Tony Manero danced and the Hunt brothers lost a large part of the family fortune, much of the world bought wholeheartedly into the allure of precious metals. What stands readily apparent in hindsight is often very difficult to discern in the moment, amidst the enthusiasm and seduction of the bubble. What convinced otherwise thoughtful investors to buy into this bubble? The answer is inflation. The 1970s stand as the defining decade of inflation in the last 100 years in the United States. A toxic combination of loose monetary policy, a generally declining dollar, oil shocks from Arab embargoes, runaway federal spending, and the Vietnam war created an era of persistent inflation and stagnant equity prices. So poor was the macro investing environment, mostly due to inflation, that the Dow Jones Industrial Average spent the entire decade churning around 1,000 points. In fact, the DJIA first touched 1,000 way back in 1966, but failed to materially eclipse that level until 1982, after inflation was again contained.

As protection against this 1970s inflation, and seeking growth in an era of equity stagnation, investors reached for gold. But in the following pages I argue that we face no such lasting, structural inflationary dangers today—in fact, quite the opposite. And further, I demonstrate how, even if inflation does present a clear and present danger in coming years, precious metals will likely disappoint as a lasting store of value, collapsing just as violently as the 1980 gold/silver bubble popped.

The Wages of Sin

The King James Version of the Bible asserts that "the wages of sin is death."[1] In 2011 America, the "wages of sin" is . . . lower wages. Meaning that the most brutal and stubborn hangovers from the leverage-induced "sin" bubbles of the first decade of the twenty-first century are persistent unemployment, global overcapacity, and concomitant stagnant wages. In fact, wages have treaded sideways even as productivity has vaulted higher, as shown in Figure 3.1.

In other words, companies, forced to grow ever-more competitive in the global, post-crisis environment, have squeezed record pro-

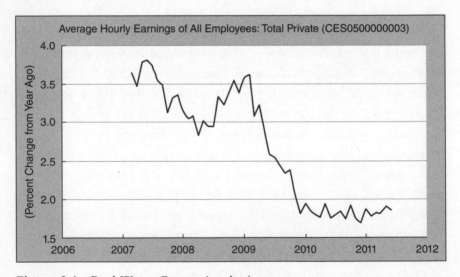

Figure 3.1 Real Wages Contracting Again
SOURCE: St. Louis Federal Reserve, U.S. Department of Labor.

ductivity out of workers, without having to share a commensurate amount of the spoils (profits) with those very workers. Persistent high joblessness and increasingly effective global outsourcing have enabled companies to press this hard bargain upon workers.

The simplest and best way to analyze this phenomenon is by watching Unit Labor Costs, meaning the cost of labor per some particular dollar value of output. Economist Steve Liesman of CNBC notes:

It is only inflationary for wages to rise if workers are not more productive. They have been very productive the past several years and yet wages have been stagnant. In the past two years, unit labor costs have fallen in five of eight quarters, including the most recent one in the fourth quarter of 2010.

So the labor component of production, all in all (including productivity) has gotten cheaper, not more expensive.[2]

Incredibly, even as food and energy costs that workers face at home have skyrocketed, and despite the federal government's consistent efforts to reflate the economy, real wages are falling. Liesman's last point is one of the most critical: that Unit Labor Costs soared in the 1970s. The Tony Manero of 2011 feels lucky to have a job at all and does not protest for higher wages, even as his productivity increases.

Figure 3.2 details the recent plunge in Unit Labor Costs.

Rising inflation results, primarily, from rising wages. David Rosenberg, chief economist for Gluskin Sheff, determined that wages and inflation correlate 88 percent of the time historically.[3] In its simplest form, too much money in consumer pockets starts to chase too few goods and services, sending prices spiraling higher. Such was certainly the case in the 1970s, as CPI, real estate, wages, and interest rates all ascended rapidly. Such is certainly not the case in the new age of deleveraging we are witnessing presently. And with real wages falling, not rising, that lack of pricing pressure is not likely to dissipate anytime soon.

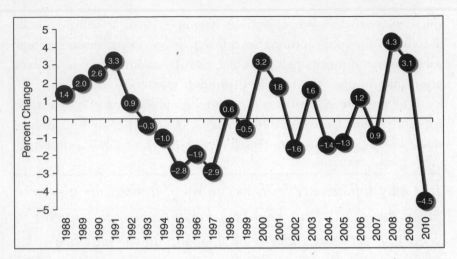

Figure 3.2 Over-the-Year Percentage Change in Unit Labor Costs, Manufacturing (1988 to 2010)
SOURCE: U.S. Bureau of Labor Statistics.

This trend of high unemployment presents, in many ways, a structural problem in joblessness unseen since the Great Depression. Recent data suggest that entire swaths of the working age population have permanently dropped out of the workforce. In 2010, only 45.4 percent of all Americans held jobs, a record low since 1983, and down from a record high a decade earlier in 2000 at 49.3 percent. Looking at men only, the situation is even graver. Historically, about 80 percent of all men work. But recently, the percentage of employed men declined to just 66.8 percent, the lowest ever. Men were hit particularly hard when the housing boom crashed, since they occupied the vast majority of construction-related jobs tied to the massive over-building bubble. The total percentage of women working has dropped too, though far less precipitously. Another frightening comparison regarding the labor market focuses on age demographics. As I mentioned in Chapter 1, America has by far the best demographic future of any developed nation. But even in America, it is worth noting that in 2000, our country had roughly an equal number of children and non-working adults. Since then, the population of non-working adults has grown by a staggering 27 million, while only 3 million new children under age 18 have been added. These trends all augur very ill for wages, and especially for real productivity-adjusted wage growth. Similar to housing, which faces a "shadow inventory" of homes not officially for sale but nonetheless waiting to be sold, the labor market has its own "shadow supply" of dropout workers. Combined with a persistently high unemployment rate, which includes only those actively looking for work, the labor situation tilts heavily in favor of employers and will do so for years to come. Such a scenario does not bode well for the hyperinflation scenarios championed by gold proponents.

Moreover, joblessness for those who are searching for work has evolved into almost a lifestyle. That is, the search is taking longer than at any time since the 1930s. The rather chilling chart in Figure 3.3 compares the longevity of unemployment in previous recessions, wherein getting back to 100 on the graph represents a full jobs recovery from the beginning of the recession.

As Figure 3.3 makes evident, a full three years after the start of this recent recession, the labor market is nowhere near reclaiming its losses, and it falls far short of the trajectory of previous recessions and recoveries. Once again, such a prolonged process does not at all support the notion that wages will rise and, hence, prices in general. And if lasting inflation does not appear likely, then the euphoria surrounding gold represents a calamitous bubble. Figure 3.4, taken from John Mauldin's excellent book *Endgame*, makes a similar point, showing the longevity of average unemployment overlaid with the falling workforce participation rate we have detailed.

Admittedly, it is self-evident that post-crisis we have indeed experienced serious commodity inflation. As the Federal Reserve embarked on two rounds of quantitative easing, essentially printing money and attempting to debase the U.S. dollar and reflate the economy, it has in actuality only succeeded in creating a very narrow form of inflation in physical commodities including, but not at all limited to, gold. This form of inflation creates enormous hardships for middle and lower

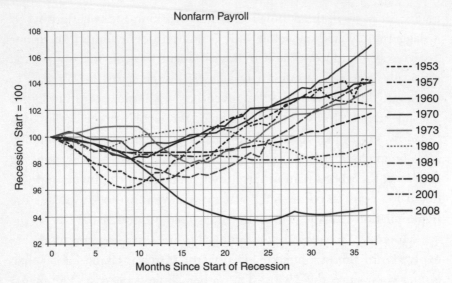

Figure 3.3 Nonfarm Payroll

NOTE: Nonfarm business sector (Productivity and Costs) = The nonfarm business sector is a subset of the domestic economy and excludes the economic activities of the following: general government, private households, nonprofit organizations serving individuals, and farms. The nonfarm business sector accounted for about 77 percent of the value of the gross domestic product (GDP) in 2000.
SOURCE: U.S. Bureau of Labor Statistics, Bloomberg Financial.

income workers, because they spend an inordinate amount of income on food and energy. And indeed, those workers have shouldered the worst burden of the Fed's QE (Quantitative Easing) policy.

The single mother waitress who drives her kids to school and then goes to her shift at a restaurant has struggled mightily to fill her gas tank, feed her children as food prices rise, and find anything at all left to spend on discretionary goods or put into savings. But the partner at a large law firm, while he may complain heartily as he pays to fill his Range Rover SUV, in point of fact changes his behavior and financial patterns little, because food and energy consume such a small percentage of his total income. He may well have more than compensated for his higher gasoline costs, as an example, from the profits he

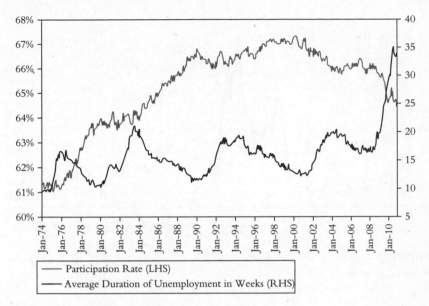

Figure 3.4 Average Duration of Unemployment and Participation Rate
Source: John Mauldin, *Endgame* (Hoboken, NJ: John Wiley & Sons, 2011). Reprinted with permission of John Wiley & Sons, Inc.

could have earned in his portfolio as an owner of energy-related company shares.

But life is not all roses in this age of deleveraging, even for the successful attorney. He could face, for example, serious price headwinds in charging his clients for legal services. Because, unlike commodities, services have been maintaining a firmly disinflationary trend, even as the recovery elongates. Figure 3.5 depicts the trend of stubbornly contained prices for the services sectors.

As evidenced on this graph, services prices soared in the 1970s, creating an eventual huge spike in gold and silver. Yet even that precious metals spike was unsustainable. Given the nature of services sector pricing pressure to the *downside* now, I find the recent "melt-up" in gold and silver even more unsustainable and dangerous. Given that more than two-thirds of the present U.S. economy consists of services,

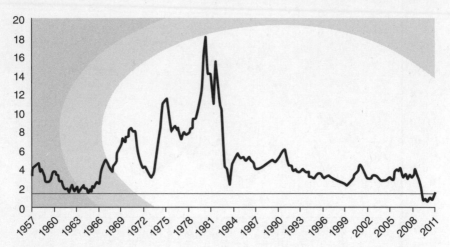

Figure 3.5 United States: Consumer Price Index: Services (year-over-year percentage change)
SOURCE: Haver Analytics, Gluskin Sheff (www.cnbc.com/id/42663205/).

this trend of downward pricing pressures stands as a very material and profound restraint upon prices in general. Even with massive government stimuli, fiscally in the form of spending/borrowing and monetarily in the form of QE, the government has been unable to get services prices off the floor. And I believe that opposition to any further QE grows apace, within Washington and throughout America, making a government-induced bout of services inflation all the more unlikely going forward.

Helicopter Ben Just Can't "Make It Rain"

This chapter about gold began by discussing a rapper, MC Hammer. Apparently, a favorite activity of rappers consists of walking into strip-tease clubs with wads of cash, throwing them in the air to "make it rain," and enjoying the ensuing pandemonium. I am not sure that Ben Bernanke, the august Federal Reserve Chairman, would approve of such activities, but he has proven totally incapable of "making it rain" in the economic sense, in spite of throwing an epic amount of cash money around.

In 2002, well before the tumultuous crisis events of 2008 and 2009, Bernanke earned the nickname "Helicopter Ben" because of a speech he gave describing the capabilities of the Fed in fighting deflation.[4] Chairman Bernanke was actually referencing Nobel economist Milton Friedman, who used the term to describe fighting a liquidity trap by dropping money on the system, as if from a helicopter. Once the housing/credit crisis was in full bloom, Helicopter Ben indeed got his chance to take the controls and take flight, showering the economy with liquidity, first by bringing the Fed Funds interest rate to 0 percent and then by two full-fledged programs of Quantitative Easing, wherein the Federal Reserve bought bonds, from Treasuries to mortgages, injecting the banking system with record amounts of capital. The intent and hope, of course, were that such injections would achieve two goals. The first, which was achieved, was to backstop the whole financial system and ensure that credit markets could function, averting a complete liquidity trap, wherein no one will extend credit, even to the most deserving borrowers. The second goal was to spur growth in credit, encouraging banks and others to lend money and create a multiplier effect, wherein each dollar injected in reality creates several dollars worth of economic activity. For example, Citibank makes a loan to the new home buyer, enticed by far lower housing prices, who then shops at Home Depot to fix up the house, convincing Home Depot to hire additional workers, who then feel free to spend money on dinner out, and pay a babysitter, and so on. But one giant problem evolved: The capital injections did not spur a serious multiplier effect. In fact, there has been extremely little velocity of money, meaning that money is not turning over much at all. Instead, the banks used the capital to deleverage, pulling back from lending. Individuals have acted much the same, using any proceeds from stimuli to pay down debts and enact personal austerity. After facing the financial abyss in 2008, few have been willing to engage in the same sort of reckless behavior. And for those who are

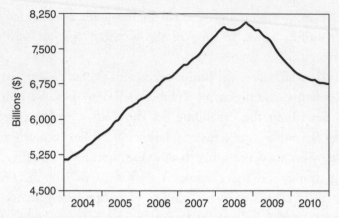

Figure 3.6 Break-Adjusted Loans and Leases in Bank Credit: All Commercial Banks SA

SOURCE: Haver Analytics (http://singapore.pimco.com/LeftNav/Featured+Market+Commentary/ FF/2011/Tony+Crescenzi+Ben+Emons+and+Lupin+Rahman+January+2011.htm), data from Federal Reserve.

willing, credit has become too scarce anyway, as credit standards from banks have overshot from nonexistent to highly restrictive. Figure 3.6 shows the declining nature of bank lending.

In this age of deleveraging and thrift, the harsh reality is that, despite the Fed's massive liquidity injections, inflation need not necessarily result if the velocity of money does not take off. Gold bugs insist that a government printing press must necessarily create rampant, structural inflation. But they neglect to acknowledge the serious evidence pointing to low or no velocity of capital, restraining general pricing even while creating inflated bubbles in isolated areas—especially gold! Helicopter Ben has, therefore, indeed showered the system with money, but he has been woefully unable to really "make it rain."

Figure 3.7 tells a similar story about the velocity of capital. This money multiplier ratio is the relationship of M1 to the St. Louis Fed Adjusted Monetary Base. It effectively represents the ratio of private commercial bank money relative to government central bank money.

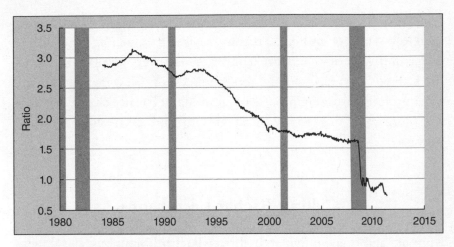

Figure 3.7   Money Multiplier
NOTE: Shaded areas indicate U.S. recessions.
SOURCE: Federal Reserve Bank of St. Louis.

The chart in the figure shows serious problems in expanding the money supply. Even when government policy is as accommodative as possible, it cannot overcome an entrenched unwillingness of the private sector to expand credit in general. This chart argues strongly that, despite the efforts of Helicopter Ben, deflation still poses a very real risk. As an analog, Japan is embarking not on QE1 or QE2, but seemingly on QE-infinity. And yet, the Bank of Japan has been unable to generate any velocity of money at all in that economy. I am not comparing the United States to Japan; as mentioned at length in Chapter 2, that country faces many problems endemic to Japan. Further, the United States possesses attributes strikingly absent in Japan, chiefly a growing population and a culture of risk. But nonetheless, Japan does offer an example, albeit an extreme one, of a scenario where easy monetary policy need not produce inflation. In fact, in Japan's case, not only has it not produced any inflation, but loose policy has not even precluded outright deflation. Simply put: Credit contraction can more than offset loose monetary policy. Japan clearly faces that predicament at present. And I believe the United States will see a similar, though less severe, trend as well in the coming years. The fears of gold bugs, therefore—talk of spiking Treasury yields, a careening lower U.S. dollar, and Weimar-republic-like inflation—are very misplaced. Instead, the United States faces a long, tough process of deleveraging. We will see a prolonged, boring process of cleansing of balance sheets, personal and corporate, marked by slow growth and even slower pricing pressures.

Calling Richard Simmons

My wife and I have often argued over Richard Simmons, the fitness/ weight loss guru of "Sweatin' to the Oldies." She sees him as a dedi- cated, enthusiastic humanitarian and coach, imploring people to reach high and achieve. I see him more as a late-night television charlatan, producing crocodile tears at the stories of obese "patients" he treats en route to his own serious wealth. Regardless, Richard has seized on a very profitable business, as we Americans clamor endlessly for methods of sustaining weight loss. Well, if Richard can coach Americans away from buffet tables and onto gym floors, perhaps he can also help cure our massive other overcapacity—of the economic variety. The excesses created by the housing and credit bubbles leading up to the 2008 crisis will take many years to dissipate and rectify. America must, and will, get fit again financially. But as with physical weight loss, there exist few easy cures. The excesses simply must be worked off. For example, take a look at Capacity Utilization (Figure 3.8), which measures the amount of industrial output that actually is produced versus the total capacity of industrial output that could be produced given existing equipment.

Although Capacity Utilization has bounced back from the 2009 lows, it still sits nowhere near the 80+ percent area that marked much of the last 25 years. A more extreme example of the overcapacity present in the economy is evident in automobiles. Presently, total auto production capacity in America stands at about 18 million vehicles,

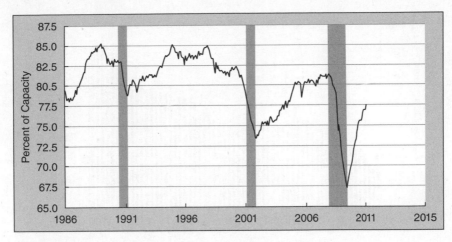

Figure 3.8 Capacity Utilization: Total Industry (TCU)
NOTE: Shaded areas indicate U.S. recessions.
SOURCE: Board of Governors, Federal Reserve System (http://research.stlouisfed.org/fred2/graph/?s[1][id]=TCU).

even though present pace indicates an annual rate of only 13.5 million vehicles actually selling. And because of China's reckless government-dictated additions to auto capacity, the global overcapacity issue in autos is equally problematic. With global capacity now rising to above 100 million vehicles per year, sales look unlikely to top 60 million. Given that level of overcapacity, and a still-depressed (though admittedly growing) rate of Capacity Utilization, the industrial scene just does not indicate that inflationary worries are well founded.

Moreover, although consumers are clearly pulling back from the high rates of indebtedness that fueled the boom into 2007, the average balance sheet—like the average waistline—still needs quite a bit more austerity. Consider Figure 3.9, which shows total debts in relation to after-tax income.

Although the trend points, finally, in the right direction, getting back to the 80 percent area that marked most of the 1980s and 1990s will take either a serious jump in income or further serious personal deleveraging, a whole lot of "Sweatin' to the Oldies." As we discussed in previous pages, with incomes stagnating, less credit will probably

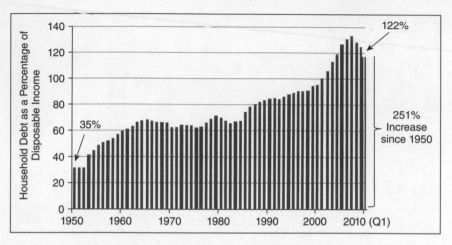

Figure 3.9 U.S. Household Debt Has Reached Historically High Levels as a Percentage of Disposable Income

SOURCES: Data from the Federal Reserve, *Flow of Funds Accounts—Liabilities of Households and Nonprofit Organizations* and Bureau of Economic Analysis, *Personal Income and Its Disposition*, February 2010. Compiled by PGPF (www.pgpf.org/Special-Topics/Personal-Responsibility-Primer.aspx?p=1).

form the only path lower on this chart, moving back nearer to normal levels. To get there, we see the savings rate also climbing back to the 10 percent levels that dominated much of the 1970s and 1980s.

Speaking of austerity, even government wants to get in on the act. Austerity at the state and local level is already a reality. Because the states cannot print their own currency, they are forced to pay real bills with real money, and to borrow without the benefits of an explicit federal government guarantee. As such, budget battles are heating up across state capitals. A look at Figure 3.10, which gives figures on real per capita expenditures in the state of Indiana, is instructive.

I see this trend spreading throughout the nation as governors and legislators make tough choices regarding pensions, state borrowing, and outlays, facing the tough discipline of more skeptical municipal bond markets. The bigger question will be: Does Washington get religion in regard to spending? I am willing to bet that austerity penetrates even the profligate halls of Washington. The 2010 mid-term elections ushered into office a backbench group of libertarian-minded Tea Party

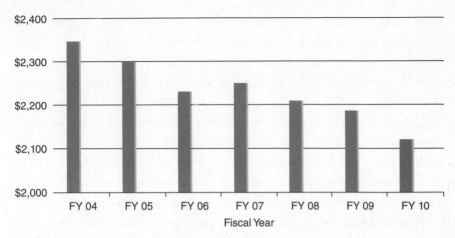

Figure 3.10 Real per Capita Expenditures
SOURCE: IN.gov.

Republicans unwilling to compromise on business as usual. Although those members do not by any stretch control the Congress, they do exert strong influence on the GOP caucus, and they look for serious austerity measures to take hold for the first time in decades. Fiscal austerity, like all other kinds of belt-tightening, is not welcome news for owners of gold.

John L. Sullivan in the Red Corner

I love the sport of boxing and its long, colorful history. Many casual observers recoil at the idea that, in the nineteenth century, all boxing was bare-knuckle. "What kind of barbarians?" would be a typical reaction. But in fact, boxing gloves do not make the act of boxing safer but instead decidedly more dangerous. They offer a false sense of protection. Yes, they do very well protect the hands. But in doing so, the gloves also afford boxers the ability to throw magnificently hard punches repeatedly to the opponent's cranium, inflicting far more damage than would be possible bare-knuckled. In fact, bare-knuckle fights focused largely on the body, since full-scale blows to the head would often result in a broken hand, meaning pain and an "L" for the bout. Spectators love the violence of gloves-required matches, but the safety of fighters would improve were they not allowed the false protection of gloves.

In similar fashion, gold offers investors a false sense of protection. Gold has been heavily marketed to mom-and-pop investors as a cure-all device. Mostly it has been sold as a defense against inflation. I clearly do not foresee inflation as a looming threat. In fact, I still see deflation as a far greater risk. But even if I am ludicrously wrong and inflation is about to take root, is gold the right insurance? The evidence on that point is spotty.

For example, if you were unlucky enough to buy gold at the 1980 highs, fearing continued 1970s-style inflation into the 1980s, and held gold through the 1999 lows at $252 an ounce, even while CPI more than doubled in those two decades, that investment in gold declined a stunning 70 percent. Clearly, I am cherry-picking an awful scenario using the highs and the lows. But using a far longer time frame, it is worth noting that in 2011, with gold at $1,400 an ounce, it still trades far lower than its inflation-adjusted high above $2,400. Many gold bulls argue that gold is headed there, and soon, but the point is that for the better part of three decades, gold has come nowhere near to protecting an investor from the corrosive effects of inflation. Using 1980 again as a reference point, but instead of starting with the $850 high, using the far fairer $400 price it also saw that year, that $400 buy was precisely unchanged a full 10 years later in 1990. In that time, though, CPI had increased 60 percent. Over the course of a decade, gold provided no insurance whatever against rising prices in general. During that same 10-year span, it also provided no protection against a falling U.S. dollar. For example, as gold grew $0, from a $400 start to a $400 finish a decade later, the dollar lost almost half its value versus the Japanese yen, descending from 200 yen per dollar all the way to 110 yen per dollar. Looking more recently at the 2008 credit crisis, gold provided not only no insurance but instead, at the very depths of the crisis, a dangerous, risky holding. As global markets melted down in October of 2008, gold actually lost 20 percent, exacerbating the losses investors were experiencing in holding anything but U.S. Treasuries. At its essence, gold was then, and is now, a very speculative bet, one primarily against the U.S. dollar. It is not, however, an insurance policy, as proven by the carnage of October 2008.

So if gold is not a reliable hedge against inflation, how then does an intelligent investor analyze gold? The unsatisfying, though brutally honest, answer is: Gold is largely unanalyzable. That is, since gold has no actual use, it remains a supremely psychologically based resource. In fact, gold stands pretty much alone as an asset in that it throws off no income, nor does it promise the possibility of income.

Gold bugs often cite the finite supply of gold as its chief asset. Considering that almost all the gold ever produced still exists, it supposedly acts as a perfect currency, an agreed upon store of value, the supply of which cannot be shrunk or expanded, as is the case with fiat currencies such as the U.S. dollar or euro currency. But this thinking falls short on two levels. First, there are other finite resources that can, and do, serve as serious stores of value to protect against inflation. The most obvious, and accessible, is real estate. Just like gold, all the land ever created still exists. It is neither created nor destroyed. But in stark contrast to gold, land produces income. Owning land inherently involves collecting rents, or at least the potential to do so. Owning gold means paying for storage and guards, and the surety that one will never collect income from the investment. Second, gold itself is actually a fiat resource itself. That is, its value is purely derived from perception. Because it has no actual use, unlike property or oil, and because it produces no income, unlike bonds, its value relies exclusively on the perception of its value, not at all dissimilar to the U.S. dollar, even though it is endlessly touted as the antidote to fiat currencies. To take this point further, I would even argue that gold is more of a fiat bet than the U.S. dollar. At least the Treasury and the Fed have an army, the most dominant in history I might add, to back the government's claims that the currency represents value and safety.

Gold flies no such flag, and is backed by no army. Admittedly, gold does find the weight of history on its side, having been deemed valuable by everyone from Hernán Cortés to MC Hammer. But the weight of history does not dismiss the reality that gold relies completely on human belief in its value, rather than functioning as a usable, income-producing asset.

On this point, it is worth noting that stocks and property have, over time, served as much better protections against inflation than gold. For example, in the late 1970s property surged as general prices rose. Owners of property enjoyed serious price appreciation and the significant income of rents, all while gold owners endured a massive bubble rally and demise. Unless the gold owners were skillful enough to sell at the 1980 highs (and stay out of the market), the owners of property—or shares or foreign currencies like the yen—were much better compensated than precious metals investors. If today an investor truly believes in inflation ahead, it is far better to buy a massive multinational company share that pays a healthy dividend and earns most of its earnings outside the United States, thereby benefiting from currency depreciation. For example, inflation worriers would be far better served buying Intel or Exxon Mobil, which derive 70+ percent of revenue from abroad, and collecting the dividend as income, than buying into a dangerously inflated gold bubble. Once again, I believe the greatest risk to the economy is still deflation, not inflation. But if I am wrong, and the inflation worries about the government printing money are in fact accurate, then gold still does not represent the soundest protection.

Three's Company

The hit ABC comedy *Three's Company* premiered the same year that Tony Manero boogeyed to the Bee Gees on the big screen. This was 1977, just as inflation really took effect. The CPI, for reference, climbed an incredible 60 percent from the beginning of that year to the end of

1981. The title of the ABC show came from the old adage that "two's company, three's a crowd." The clear implication of the saying is that crowds should be avoided. As mentioned in the introduction, I have never forgotten the sage wisdom of the Las Vegas sports book teller who told me—rather dryly—that "the masses . . . are asses." On a more ominous note, the *SS Eastland* disaster proved the very tangible danger of crowd behavior, drowning hundreds of people in only feet of water because of the herd action of a group. Whether watching Jack Tripper on reruns or reading about the poor laborers and families that perished on the *Eastland*, the message of history rings unmistakably—that mass crowd movements should be analyzed with the most discerning and skeptical mindsets.

In present-day investing, I can think of no more crowded, herd-like trade than the bullish gold theme. This idea has become so accepted, such a common narrative among investors, that the inherent danger of its crowded nature has become obscured and difficult to ascertain. But the maverick investor, wary of the madness of crowds, needs to think independently and rationally and avoid the pitfalls of crowd behavior, and perhaps even profit from the inevitable reckonings such bubbles compel.

Just how crowded is the gold trade? According to the *Financial Times*, about 50 percent of the existing stock of mined gold is preserved as a pure store of value, for investment purposes only.[5] Expounding on this point, the *Wall Street Journal* reports that "historically investors accounted for a relatively small portion of gold demand, with the majority driven by the needs of jewelers, dentists, and electronics manu-facturers. In 1998, investors represented [just] 6.9 percent of demand, in the second quarter of 2010 investors accounted for [a staggering] 51 percent."[6] Once investors account for more demand for a product than actual end consumers, the crowd is clearly leaning very hard, creating untold dangers. Similar behavior was evident at the height of the real estate bubble in the Sun Belt, with nonresident owners flipping unbuilt condos in Miami and Las Vegas for serious profits well before a con-struction shovel ever touched the dirt.

Interestingly, Warren Buffett, the most successful investor in history, eschews gold for this very reason of crowded perception, saying, "Gold gets dug out of the ground in Africa, or someplace. Then we melt it down, dig another hole, bury it again and pay people to stand around guarding it. It has no utility. Anyone watching from Mars would be scratching their head."[7] In other words, gold relies purely on the sentiment of the crowd, a most specious foundation. Another legendary investor, George Soros, stated at the 2011 Davos World Economic Summit that "gold is an ultimate asset bubble." He pointed out that gold, like most asset bubbles, begins with some logical thinking. With the Federal Reserve recklessly providing credit, people instinctively reached for private stores of value, from corporate bonds to commodities. And gold, given its millennia-long track record as a desired commodity, rightly saw serious inflows. But like all bubbles, the original rationale soon subsided and animal instincts took over, driving the price of gold to utterly unsustainable levels. We find an analog in the late 1990s technology bubble. The first capital inflows found serious justification as the Internet and telecom changed drastically the daily lives of millions of consumers and businesses. But eventually, the easy money provided by an excessively easy Fed (sound familiar?) was food for a beast that grew out of control until the tech bubble burst with a massive pop in the spring of 2000.

Like TheGlobe.com and other assets of those halcyon Silicon Valley glory days, gold too finds its value is predicated on the "greater fool" theory. And for gold, the prospects are even worse. At least investors in TheGlobe.com expected cash flow at some point. Owners of gold are betting merely on the belief (hope) that, despite its utter lack of utility, some other person (fool) will be willing to pay a yet-higher price for the same shiny sentimental object. Such practices can clearly work with artwork—in fact, they work amazingly well. But that game is best played by the super rich, not regular investors, and no serious analyst would argue that a Picasso is an asset class, even given a long-standing perception of value.

An Asset for All Seasons

Sir Thomas More, a saint of the Catholic Church, was immortalized in the famous play and Academy Award-winning movie *A Man for All Seasons*. Thomas More sacrificed a life of esteem and success as Lord Chancellor of England when he refused to comply with King Henry VIII's split from the Roman Church, and eventually he paid with his life. His contemporaries called him a man for "all seasons," meaning that he thrived in all environs and found value and meaning in all circumstances. To listen to the gold crowd of 2011, gold has become the Thomas More of investments. That is, gold thrives in every environment. It represents insurance against inflation, but does just fine in deflation too as a safety mechanism. The gold bugs also postulate that gold ascends with dollar debasement and the concomitant inflationary asset rise, but amazingly also profits from retrenchment and austerity.

Respected gold analyst Eugen Weinberg at the giant German bank Comerzbank recently wrote: "Either a swift economic recovery or further dismal economic performance should bring new buyers into the market . . . a strong economy would create more jewelry demand. If the economy stays weak or gets worse, then investors will be looking for a safe haven."[8] Call me skeptical, but once the crowd starts to say "heads we win . . . oh, and tails we win too," then my maverick contrarian radar starts to flash serious warnings.

Truly Can't (Won't) Touch This

No matter what my heritage, I will staunchly turn my back on any Conquistador lineage, real or exaggerated, and resist the allure of the yellow metal. And despite the melodious entreaties of MC Hammer, his kind of marketing too will fail to command my investment and belief in gold. First and foremost, because the world still faces a serious risk of deflation, not inflation, especially in developed, services-dominated economies like the United States. Second, because gold represents a poor and dangerous form of protection against the ravages of inflation, even if the threat of broad price increases were credible. And finally, because the gold trade is perhaps the most crowded investment theme of my career as a trader and analyst. For these reasons, I will not invest in the gold scheme.

I also will not wear those ridiculous baggy pants favored by MC Hammer, but that is probably a less controversial position.

Chapter 4

House of Pain

Housing Does Not Recover Anytime Soon

W ay back, during my college days in the early 1990s, a rap band from Los Angeles named House of Pain came to fame. In fact, in 1992 and 1993, it seems I heard their song "Jump Around" everywhere I traversed, from our football locker room, to bars, to boom boxes playing on the quad (yes, before the digital music age people still carried boom boxes with CDs and even cassettes). The triumphal lyrics boasted of the crème de la crème rising to the heights. Of course then no one was concerned with housing prices or, for that matter, the price of much except for beer and burritos. But like cream rising, asset prices in general were just beginning to rise from the 1991 recession.

After I graduated and went to work in the Treasury bond market as a broker, I marveled at the rally I witnessed in housing starting in the mid-1990s. That rally took a very brief pause around the demise of the tech bubble in 2000 and September 11, 2001, but then launched into overdrive, producing price gains that dwarfed the rally of the late 1990s. Of course, the subsequent blowup in housing, which commenced in 2007, triggered a global financial crisis unseen since the Great Depression. We are, very much, still in the midst of that crisis. As I study the housing market today in 2011, despite four years of wrenching corrections, I foresee far more pain ahead and indeed a very long slog before housing can truly reach the ever-elusive bottom. And as such, I also project opportunities for the independent-minded investor both to profit and to avoid perils as the housing decline persists. Considering the factors weighing on a housing recovery, the reality of the property markets still signals a "House of Pain" in the months and years ahead.

Can We Protect This House?

Anyone who watches NFL football on television in recent years has seen the near-ubiquitous Under Armour commercials in which gladiatoresque, Under Armour-clad football players declare "we must protect this house!" Indeed the ethos of "home" plays a central role in American culture, as evidenced by phrases like "a man's home is his castle." For almost 100 years, the federal government has pursued policies in alignment with Under Armour's advertisements, believing at all times that "we (the taxpayer) must protect this house." But should home ownership be a universally supported societal goal? And more to the point of this book, does this long-standing bias in favor of owning homes make investment sense right now, in 2011?

As a contrarian thinker, my answer to both questions is a resounding "no." But before we analyze the present and projected future state of housing, a look backward proves helpful, in understanding how the housing market arrived at this most unfortunate juncture. As such, I will assail the myriad distortions created by government intervention in housing, describe the giant profits realized by one maverick investor willing to bet "against the house," present the hurdles still facing housing, and then prescribe a strategy for facing the future of housing.

The Visible Hand

As a young boy when our family went to visit my grandmother on her Indiana farm, I hated two things about those visits. First, I found out how hard farm work was, particularly when it involved cleaning up barns and stalls, as there is simply no way to make animal waste exciting (or a pleasant olfactory experience). The second reason is that my grandmother would serve us, as snack, free cheese she got from the government, I believe as part of an elderly-assistance program. As anyone could guess, government cheese tasted terrible, and was (is) undoubtedly a testimony to the power of the dairy lobby rather than Washington's skill in food processing.

The same could be said for government housing. Few, if any, people desire to live in government housing (especially if they have to eat government cheese in that abode!). But alas, few Americans realize that, to some degree, we all live in government housing. That is, the scope and degree of government involvement in the allegedly private housing market would astound citizens of this mostly capitalist country. And, as is so often the case, at the root of the housing bubble and implosion, the crime scene is indeed littered with the handprints of the federal government.

Long before government cheese, Adam Smith spoke 250 years ago of the "invisible hand" alive in capitalism that guided, without central control, an economy toward its maximum potential. He argued that countless self-interested actors would create, if left largely unfettered, a remarkable harmony and productivity, appearing on the macro level as if a magical hand was orchestrating the efforts from above. In the case of housing in America, sadly, the very *visible* hand of government, through the best of intentions, created a bubble such as our nation has never experienced before.

Although Washington has been too involved in housing for many decades, the real culprit of our present morass is the Community Reinvestment Act of 1977 (CRA). Like most government intrusions into the private sector, despite the eventual havoc created by the visible hand of government, the CRA was indeed spawned from noble intentions. Like Dr. Frankenstein in the Mary Shelley classic, the experiment was not born of ill intent, but quickly devolved, creating a monster. Specifically, the CRA sought to redress discriminatory credit practices, particularly those marginalizing low-income neighborhoods in which banks redlined whole communities as not creditworthy. The CRA required that all banks meet the credit needs of low-income and minority constituencies in which the institutions are chartered. To enforce the Act, the CRA empowered regulatory bodies to oversee compliance and, most importantly, made applications for new branches and mergers and acquisitions dependent upon a bank's degree of CRA conformity.

At the outset the CRA was not an overly obtrusive or burdensome statute. But, like many statutes, its final impact derived not so much from the language at inception, but rather from its eventual implementation at the regulatory and judicial levels. John Carney correctly describes its evolution:

The CRA was not a static piece of legislation. It evolved over the years from a relatively hands-off law focused on process into one that focused on outcomes. Regulators, beginning in the mid-nineties, began to hold banks accountable in serious ways. Banks responded to this new accountability by increasing the CRA loans they made, a move that entailed relaxing their lending standards.[1]

Indeed, for most of the 1980s, the CRA gathered dust as an ignored and that unimportant law. But starting in 1989, in the wake of the mammoth Savings and Loan crisis, President George H.W. Bush signed the Financial Institutions Reform, Recovery, and Enforcement Act, which made CRA compliance for banks far more public and demanding. As a result, present Federal Reserve Chairman Ben Bernanke wrote that advocacy groups were enabled to "perform more-sophisticated, quantitative analyses of banks' records"[2] and thereby ensured much additional political pressure to extend credit, regardless of the actual economic merits of said credit. Then in 1993, newly elected President Bill Clinton greatly expanded the reach of the CRA by commanding regulators to spur an ever-greater expansion of credit. According to his economic aide Robert Rubin, the CRA enhancements aimed to "deal with the problems of the inner city and distressed rural communities."[3] Though signed by Democrat President Jimmy Carter and expanded by Democrat Bill Clinton, Republicans were all too willing to play politics with the balance sheets of private banks. In 2002, President George W. Bush said in a speech at the St. Paul AME Church in Atlanta, GA, "We certainly don't want there to be fine print preventing people from owning their home . . . we can change the print, and we've got to." He also stated that "we want everybody in America to own their own home, that is what we want." Well, be careful what you wish for. Although an ownership society makes for good campaign script, the harsh reality is that home ownership, as we will examine in the coming pages of this chapter, should not at all be a universal goal. Nor does widespread ownership of risky assets—as we now know housing to be—create a more stable society.

And the intrusion into housing and mortgage lending was not confined to regulatory and statutory rules. No, the federal government made very certain that banks would and could expand credit, commensurate with the spirit of the CRA, because federal agencies, primarily Fannie Mae and Freddie Mac were, in fact, at the behest of Housing and Urban Development (HUD) secretary Cuomo, during the Clinton Administration, willing to purchase up to $2 trillion of "affordable" mortgages. So on one hand, the banks were badgered into lending to people and communities based on income (meaning low) and location (meaning poor), rather than based on creditworthiness and sound real estate experience. On the other hand, though, the federal government did stand ready to purchase giant tranches of these risky mortgages, which were bundled together or "securitized" and then sold to Fannie and Freddie, which enjoyed the de facto backing of the full faith and credit of the American taxpayer.

Given this two-headed monster—government pressure to make risky loans and then government promises to buy these loans once securitized—it is really little wonder that banks and the real estate business embarked on a credit binge of epic proportions. With some help from Washington, gone were the days of 30 percent down payments, verification of income, and requisite high credit scores. Instead, "liar loans" abounded, promising credit in exchange for a pulse, and pushing lending into areas previously excluded, meaning no down payment, low credit scores, and "no doc" applications requiring little (or no) verification of the borrower's assertions. In fact, as late as 2007, even as the cracks in the housing and mortgage markets became readily apparent, Fed Chairman Ben Bernanke suggested further increasing the involvement of Fannie and Freddie in the affordable housing market, urging them to facilitate the securitization of even more CRA loans, promising—quite incredibly—that "these loans usually do not involve disproportionately higher levels of default."[4]

Throughout the 1990s and into the first decade of the twenty-first century, the federal government inserted itself boldly into the previously private mortgage markets, dictating the terms of origination and guaranteeing a secondary market for resale of those same loans. And while the goals of that insertion were—and still may be—laudable, that is, encouraging an ownership society of stakeholders, the unavoidable reality is that federal involvement created the conditions for a bubble of epic scope that, in reality, does far more damage to the financial health of America than any perceived socially engineered good originally intended. The problem lies, primarily, in incentives, perverted ones in the case of the government. In its report on the crisis, the American Enterprise Institute wrote correctly that:

Unlike an insurance company, the government has no profit incentive to price for risk, and because risk pricing can seem arbitrary and unrelated to current conditions, the government has many incentives to avoid the political controversy that risk pricing entails.[5]

In other words, to accurately price risk, the government would have to purposefully discriminate among its citizens, even if that discrimination finds basis in objective criteria, like verified income and credit scores. But for government, such discrimination represents a political impossibility (though a financial prerequisite for sound credit).

Given the staggering losses, both private and public, one might surmise that the government is scaling back on its machinations in housing. The reality, sadly, is that federal involvement in housing is actually *growing*. The federal government, through Government Sponsored Enterprises (GSEs), now backs about 90 percent of all mortgages originated.[6] Even more incredible, the taxpayers' exposure to Fannie and Freddie is now completely open-ended. That is, the GSEs have an open credit line with the Treasury Department, and capital is injected every quarter to cover losses. As of February 2011, the total tab to taxpayers was $153 billion and the Congressional Budget Office estimates the total losses through 2020 will reach a staggering $400 billion.

In March 2010, long after the overwhelmingly adverse effects of federal mortgage manipulation were well known, President Obama's Treasury Secretary Timothy Geithner had the temerity to pontificate that "there is a strong economic case . . . for preserving, designing some form of guarantee by the government to help facilitate a stable housing finance market."[7] Sure, Mr. Secretary, since the first experiment with GSEs worked so well, let's have another run at it, shall we? While you're at it, Mr. Secretary, why not send some liquor to patients at the Betty Ford Clinic? A little "hair of the dog" might be a grand idea?

A Shot to the Privates

Because of the government's ongoing distortions and encroachments upon the housing market, the private mortgage market has ceased to function at all. And without a real, thriving private credit market in housing, no stable, lasting base in housing prices will form. Christopher Whalen of Institutional Risk Analytics sagely observed, "Unless and until we fix the private mortgage securitization market, the housing market will not stabilize and the chance of further deflation will remain a threat."[8] But as long as the federal government controls such wide swaths of banking and backs such a gargantuan proportion of all new mortgages, as evidenced by Figure 4.1, the mortgage credit business will remain, de facto, a government program, and a very poorly run one at that![9]

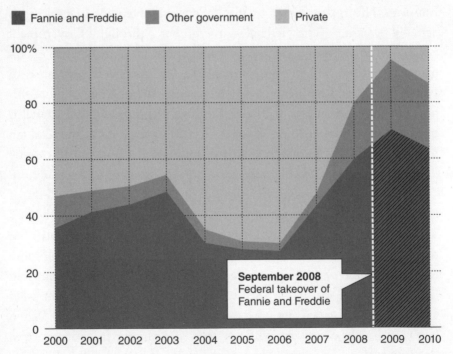

Figure 4.1 The Mortgage Market on Life Support
SOURCE: Inside Mortgage Finance. Alyson Hurt/NPR.

Moreover, government intrusion finds few barriers when it comes to mortgages. For example, the government also mandated mortgage modification efforts upon banks, attempting to deter mass foreclosures. But the results point to the inane ineffectiveness of the government's efforts. Of all loans modified by the end of 2009, almost half had the monthly payments lowered by 20 percent or more, yet by the end of 2010, a full 32 percent of those modified loans were once again delinquent (meaning payments were at least 60 days late). Moreover, of the roughly 170,000 distressed borrowers who have undergone government sponsored loan modification, over half now still sit seriously underwater on their homes, meaning that they maintain negative equity of at least 25 percent. That is, for every $1 their home is worth, they still owe at least $1.25.[10] That data actually underestimates the severity of the problem, as second-lien junior debts do not figure into that calculation. And the Administration admits that about half of all at-risk mortgages also have second liens, mostly home equity lines of credit.

Later in this chapter, I detail the incredibly dangerous degree of underwater mortgages. But for now, suffice it to say that increasingly alarming numbers of borrowers, despite the efforts of the government, face serious incentives to simply wash their hands of their house, and debt, and walk away. For both borrowers and lenders, this whole foray into "all for credit . . . and credit for all" has left a trail of tears.

The Big Short: The Doctor Makes a House Call

But some astute contrarians shed no tears when considering the destruction of recent years in mortgages and housing. Hedge fund titans like John Paulson and Kyle Bass made generational fortunes by betting often and early against the lunacy of the subprime market. Those who follow financial markets are mostly familiar with names like Bass and Paulson, which are well covered in the pages of the *Wall Street Journal* and appear on CNBC. But unless one reads Michael Lewis's book *The*

Big Short, the name Michael Burry probably does not ring a bell. Burry is a physician by training, a reclusive introvert afflicted with Asperger's syndrome. Earlier and more clearly than anyone, he foresaw the mortgage meltdown and took incredible action to capitalize from it. Sitting alone in his northern California office, with relatively limited capital in his hedge fund, he saw risks others could not. Indeed, he quite literally saw the whole world differently, because as a boy he had lost his left eye from an operation to remove a tumor from his head. Brilliant but painfully awkward, he dove into academic subjects with obsessive determination. During and after medical care he focused more on financial markets than science, before finally leaving a prestigious medical fellowship at Stanford to pursue markets full-time.

This doctor made a giant house call. In his May 2003 letter to his investors, Burry wrote,

---

You have to watch for the level at which even nearly unlimited or unprecedented credit can no longer drive the [housing] market higher . . . I am extremely bearish and feel the consequences could easily be a 50 percent drop in residential real estate in the U.S. . . . A large portion of current demand at current prices would disappear if only people became convinced that prices weren't rising. The collateral damage is likely to be orders of magnitude worse than anyone now considers.[11]

By 2005, he began to put his money where his mouth was (actually his keystrokes, as he rarely talked to anyone, preferring e-mail and letters). He actually convinced Wall Street firms, mostly Goldman Sachs and Deutsche Bank, to create credit default swaps (CDS) on mortgages. These swaps are not actually swaps at all, but rather tradable private insurance policies against default, in this case defaults of thousands of similar mortgages bundled together and sold as one security. Dr. Burry, instead of scouring medical charts and lab results, became a forensic expert of sorts on the subprime mortgage markets, identifying precisely the very worst-in-breed groups of mortgages, based on income (or lack thereof), credit scores, geography, loan to value ratios, and the like. Michael Lewis describes Burry as performing the mundane yet pivotal "old fashioned bank credit analysis on the home loans that should have been done before they were made. He was the opposite of an old fashioned banker, however. He was looking not for the best loans to make but the worst loans—so that he could bet against them." He bet against them by purchasing the CDS insurance from the Wall Street broker/dealers. He realized that this insurance was massively underpriced, and he then captured a limited-risk method to profit from the ensuing collapse of the subprime mortgage market. Note, he was not insuring any actual interest, his fund did not own any mortgages or lend at all, but rather using the insurance as a speculative means to profit from the downside of instruments that were very difficult, or impossible, to simply outright short. And at first, the Wall Street firms were all too happy to collect the fees, believing, like most of America, that housing, which had not corrected on a sustained national basis since the 1930s, was impervious to broad declines.

In fact, in October 2006, the respected, eminent chief economist of Goldman Sachs, Jan Hatzius, stated that "the point of maximum deterioration in housing activity has probably passed."[12] In point of fact, the credit train was just then approaching the true precipice of maximum danger, and Dr. Michael Burry was about to become a very wealthy man. For the purposes of this book, it is vital to recognize just how very lonely and isolated his position was in the early days. By definition, a bubble enraptures the imagination of the masses, and even the elites, who should supposedly know better. In 2005, the sharpest traders in the world at Goldman Sachs and Deutsche Bank were more than willing to sell this quirky, unknown California fund manager insurance on tranches of mortgages. But Burry proved that a maverick investor, willing to question and think about the zeitgeist of the financial age, can at times spot danger far ahead of the herd, and profit. He argued in 2005 that "it is ludicrous to believe that asset bubbles can only be recognized in hindsight . . . there are specific identifiers that are entirely recognizable during the bubble's inflation. One hallmark of mania is the rapid rise in the incidence and complexity of fraud . . . the FBI reports that mortgage-related fraud is up fivefold since 2000."[13] Similarly today, the China bubble claims adherents across wide swaths of American society, from the clerk at the 7-11 who fears that China will end American superpower dominance to the Fortune 500 CEO who pins his whole company's growth strategies on the misplaced promises of a corrupt, faltering regime in Beijing. And as I mentioned in the first chapter, the examples of securities fraud grow apace for Chinese companies.

Turning back to Dr. Michael Burry, the tide really began, in fact, to turn his way once Wall Street started noticing that much larger funds, like John Paulson's, were copying his strategies. Then, in turn, the dealers themselves began to mimic his trades, particularly Greg Lippman at Deutsche Bank, who used the massive balance sheet of his firm to replicate Burry's trades in far larger size. In doing so, Deutsche Bank flipped sides, from acting originally as "the house," allowing the relatively small player Burry to place bets, to reversing and actually joining him at the table, piggybacking Burry's bets, only using many more chips. By the time the whole subprime market collapse unfolded, Burry profited an astounding $725 million for his investors and over $100 million personally.

Admittedly, betting against housing now in 2011 will not yield anywhere near the historic returns garnered by early visionaries like Burry, Lippmann at Deutsche, and John Paulson. But the maverick, independent-minded investor can still profit from standing against the herd in housing—or at least avoid risky, costly mistakes. Specifically, the view that housing is bottoming now utterly dominates Wall Street thinking, as well as the mass media and Washington corridors of power. In fact, even John Paulson's funds have started making mammoth bets *in favor* of housing. He stated in October 2010: "If you don't own a home, buy one . . . if you own one home, buy another one, and if you own two homes buy a third and lend your relatives the money to buy a home."[14] Clearly, the consensus view has evolved into "it really can't get any worse, right?"

Wrong! Yes, it can—and likely will—get far worse. The government, through its continued machinations is, in fact, worsening and delaying the real eventual bottoming process for housing. And the risks, while clearly not as pronounced as in 2005, still point to further downside. The following hurdles, which I explore in the following pages, present formidable challenges for housing in the coming years:

- Lack of inflation
- Extent of underwater borrowers
- Poor credit availability, especially from private sources
- Massive housing supply
- Decline in household formation
- Increased awareness of the benefits of renting

"That '70s Show"

In 1998 the Fox television network found a hit in its series *That '70s Show*. Set in a small Wisconsin town in 1976, the show focused on teenage lives in the 1970s, both parodying some of the eccentricities of the 1970s as well as seriously examining such social issues as feminism and economic hardships. One recurring prop of the show was the "Stupid Helmet," an old Green Bay Packers football helmet, which characters had to don after committing some unintelligent act. As a rabid Chicago Bears fan, wearing a Packers helmet for even a moment would prove tortuous for me, indeed. In regard to housing and our present economic situation, the almost unanimous opinion, from Wall Street to Main Street, postulates that inflation is building and inevitable given our government policies. But at times the masses, and even the elites, don their own Stupid Helmets and fail to see the harsh economic realities. And the present reality indicates that prices will not approach anything like the inflationary days that marked the time of *That '70s*

Show. Instead, for reasons we touched on in Chapter 3 and for reasons I will lay out in the following pages, inflation is likely to remain extremely subdued in the months and years ahead. If anything, the risks in prices still tilt toward disinflation, meaning slower inflation, if not deflation, meaning actually net lower prices in aggregate.

This inflation argument stands at the center of prognostications on housing because many, if not most, housing bulls are counting on government-induced inflation raising the prices of real estate broadly. I will concede that if an investor believes in inflation, then property does represent a smart bet, much smarter than gold. Like gold, property is not destroyed—its supply is finite. And like gold, it is tangible. But unlike precious metals, property earns income through rent, and thus pays an inherent dividend. And indeed real estate did well in the late 1970s as prices rose generally. But the environment we face now differs greatly from the 1970s.

The simplest and most profound difference is that prices are simply *not* rising. Despite oil prices reaching above $100 per barrel twice in recent years (2008 and 2011), and despite gold reaching $1,900 per ounce and silver $50 per ounce in 2011, the reality is that broad measures of prices are barely upticking. And the main reason is that services pricing power is extremely muted. That is, the far larger and more important services components of our economy are showing little to no inflation. A combination of globalization, including outsourcing of services to places like India, and weak demand has created an environment of restrained prices for lawyers, accountants, retailers, engineers, restaurants, and so on. In stark contrast to the double-digit inflation readings of the Stupid Helmet days of the 1970s, core inflation readings today remain very tepid. As Figure 4.2 shows, core CPI is in fact trending aggressively *lower*. And core CPI, not including shelter, is trending even lower. The days of inflation running far higher than housing inflation are over, as Figure 4.2 indicates, and that portends lower prices broadly for, frankly, everything.

Looking at the Bureau of Labor Statistics CPI Shelter Index (Figure 4.3) is revelatory as well. It depicts that, while shelter costs are rising

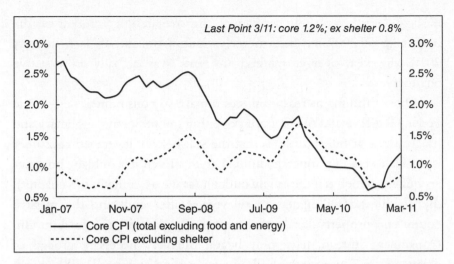

Figure 4.2 Core CPI and Core CPI Not Including Shelter (year–over–year percentage change)

SOURCE: Bureau of Labor Statistics.

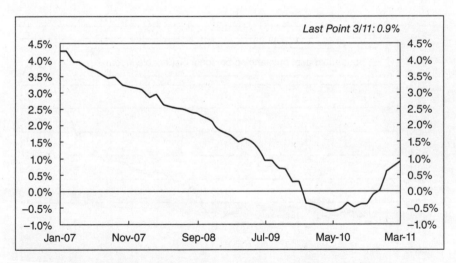

Figure 4.3 CPI Shelter Index (year–over–year percentage change)

SOURCE: Bureau of Labor Statistics.

modestly from very depressed lows, the overarching trend since the beginning of 2007 has been fiercely noninflationary. In fact, in early 2010, the year-over-year trend in rents was actually in negative territory.

One of the major reasons prices remain so constrained, despite the Federal Reserve and the Congress opening the respective monetary and fiscal spigots at full throttle, is that the still heavily leveraged consumer is unable to take on much additional credit. Even if would-be borrowers qualify, which is increasingly difficult (as we examine in this chapter), the ability and willingness to releverage after enduring the massive equity and property losses of the recent crisis continues to diminish. Consumers, instead, have only begun the very necessary process of deleveraging. This process, both unexciting and elongated, still requires far less credit—or far higher incomes—to reach any semblance of historic norms. Figure 4.4 shows that deleveraging has indeed com-

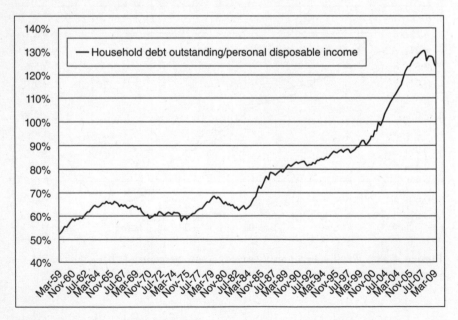

Figure 4.4   Household DTI Ratio
SOURCE: Federal Reserve, BEA.

menced, with DTI peaking in 2007 at 131 percent. But to reach even the still elevated levels of the height of the tech bubble, that ratio needs to decline all the way to below 100 percent, indicating a staggering amount of painful de-risking still ahead.

Such deleveraging does not form the kindling for an inflationary fire. Instead, the hangover from the debt binge in fact projects pricing danger to the downside, not the upside. As I discussed in Chapter 3, even infinite amounts of money printing by the government does not necessarily produce inflation, unless the velocity of that excess capital increases too. Japan represents a perfect example as they have been printing money for 20 years with the loosest of monetary policies in history, and yet the deflationary beast grows stronger. As I argued in this book's Japan chapter, thankfully America differs greatly from Japan, but nonetheless the example that loose policy *must* compel inflation is disproven mightily by studying Japan. And even here in America, the velocity of money in America is descending. So, proinflationary arguments in favor of a housing recovery rest on faulty thinking about general prices.

It's Not Raining (Working) Men

One of the reasons for the deleveraging evident in Figure 4.4 is a very troubled labor market. As I mentioned, one other way to lower the DTI, which would not require deleveraging by consumers, would be serious growth in incomes. But that growth is badly lagging as unemployment persists and the workforce shrinks dramatically as discouraged workers (or would-be workers) simply leave the world of work. For example, in 2010 only 45.4 percent of Americans had jobs, the lowest rate since 1983, and down from a peak of 49.3 percent in the year 2000.

Even worse, fewer men are working today than at any time in American history. In 1982, the Weather Girls recorded their biggest hit, "It's Raining Men." If the Weather Girls presently ran an employment agency, they would not need an umbrella, as men have gone on strike regarding employment. In 2010, only 66.8 percent of men were working. Until the 1960s, over 80 percent of men worked. Men have been leaving the workforce for decades, partly in response to women entering at an even higher rate, but the pace of male participation decline accelerated during the recent crisis, I believe, largely because of the drop in . . . you guessed it . . . housing construction!

Ring of Fire

Traveling further back in music history to 1963, Johnny Cash found one of the biggest hits of his career in the song "Ring of Fire." Sadly, housing and the job markets have entered a sort of ring of fire, wherein the circular co-dependency has created an exacerbated downturn in each. That is, housing fed the payroll gains of the late 1990s and into 2007. One of the main reasons America saw nearly full employment was that workers—especially unskilled men—could readily find employment in housing construction and related fields. And that full employment, in turn, led to even more housing demand, especially given the nearly ubiquitous availability of credit, thanks to the market interventions of the federal government. A powerful, though ultimately unsustainable, virtuous circle forged higher with housing and employment augmenting each other. The problem lies in the reverse process, which now unfolds, and on a global basis. From places as disparate as the Nevada desert to the mossy hills of Ireland, the construction recession and joblessness are feeding off each other in a circular ring of fire that, like the song, continues to burn, burn, burn. *U.S. News and World Report* editor Mort Zuckerman made this very point, writing, "We are building a million plus fewer homes on an annual basis from the peak years of the housing boom. With five people or more working on each home, we have permanently lost over 5 million jobs in residential construction."[15] And as Figure 4.5 on housing starts portrays, looking all the way back

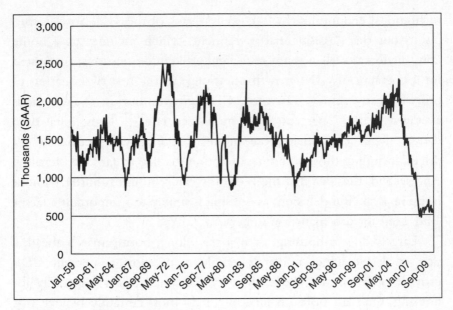

Figure 4.5   New Housing Starts
SOURCE: U.S. Census Bureau, Bloomberg.

50 years, construction has literally fallen off a cliff and shows no signs
yet of a real rebound.

The codependent spiral downward, then, between construction and
employment, emphatically argues against any lasting structural inflation.
And so, bullish bets on a macro property inflationary rebound appear
very vulnerable indeed.

Housing bulls often argue, though, that despite its clear impact on
employment, housing is simply not that important to the overall
American economy now, because the massive $6.9 trillion that
Americans have lost in housing wealth over the past six years has
greatly reduced its percentage of the overall economy. The diminished
percentage is certainly staggering, for at the 2005 peak housing construction represented 6.2 percent of GDP and has now fallen to 2.4
percent.[16] But the bulls miss an important historical truth, which is that
housing typically *leads* the economy out of recession. The idea that the
broad economy can recover as housing's woes deepen flies in the face

of historical economics. In fact, Kelly Evans of the *Wall Street Journal* points out that "Residential investment, which includes new home construction as well as renovations and broker commissions, accounted for 19 percent of GDP growth on average in the first two quarters of postwar recoveries. . . . In turn, GDP growth during those periods averaged nearly 7 percent at an annualized rate."[17] Thus, I see twin dangers here. First, that loose monetary policy will necessarily lift prices, including those of homes, a notion that has so far failed terribly. And second, the idea that the economy can rebound robustly without housing, a fanciful delusion, as housing is simply too important a factor (and asset) for too many consumers.

Largely due to housing, then, I see a long, boring march ahead; a slog of deleveraging, uncertain employment, slow 2 percent GDP growth (at best), and above all, very contained prices, especially for housing. One last note on inflation: I do most certainly believe that many emerging market countries face a formidable battle with inflation, particularly China. Those countries, unintended victims of our QE policies here in the United States, have struggled mightily to contain food prices. For smokestack economies like China, which still does not produce enough value-added goods, and very few services, the 2010 and 2011 rallies in the prices of physical inputs have placed emerging economies in a perilous spot—one reason we disbelieve in the whole emerging market lovefest. But here in America, and in the rest of the developed world, not only are price pressures tame, but in fact the real risk still lies in a tilt toward deflation.

Underwater People

The band called The Samples titled their third album *Underwater People* back in 1992, long before the mortgage crisis, and far before the term "underwater" became most commonly used not at all in reference to things aquatic, but rather to things financial. The Samples band name reportedly came from their early starving-artist days in Boulder,

Colorado, where they survived largely by eating the free samples offered by supermarkets. If my predictions about housing's continuing struggles are anywhere close to accurate, then supermarkets better rethink offering so many free samples, because lines of underwater mortgage people might well start inundating those freebie-food tables in days to come. The frightening degree of low to negative house equity presents another huge hurdle to any lasting housing recovery and, in fact, argues for much more downside before housing can reach a very elusive true "clearing" price, wherein the price has gotten so low that capital will finally soak up the mammoth supply of existing housing.

An underwater borrower is simply a homeowner who owes more in mortgage debt than the present value of his or her home. According to CoreLogic Inc, a widely followed California real estate information company, at the end of 2010, 11 million U.S. homes were underwater. An additional 2.4 million homes had less than 5 percent positive equity, meaning even a slight decrease in prices would force them too into the ranks of the underwater people. Amazingly, these two categories together account for 28 percent of all residences with mortgages.[18] So more than one out of four mortgages nationally have no or very little equity in their home. Even worse, consider the effects of a large further decrease in prices, something which, incidentally, most large banks, who hold millions of mortgages still, have not truly modeled. If housing were to drop another 5 to 10 percent, which I think is a very conservative estimate of possible downside, that further decline would bring the total peak-to-valley housing decline to 40 percent off record highs, and submerge an astounding 40 percent of all mortgages into negative equity.[19] CoreLogic also points out that 46 percent of all mortgages presently have 20 percent or less positive equity in their homes. So in truth, only half of all borrowers can withstand a substantial further decline in home prices. Such vulnerability is unprecedented in America since the Great Depression. And yet, given the feel-good equity market rally that commenced with the Federal Reserve's Quantitative Easing, Part II in August 2010, complacency regarding these risks reigns nearly uncontested. But the self-directed, independently minded investor must question the assumptions of Wall Street, the media, and Washington. After all, those supposed experts applauded the housing rally all the way to the edge of the cliff—and did some cheerleading once the descent had become evident. Should we now listen to their Pollyanna predictions of imminent recovery? No, in fact the maverick investor must consider the risks (and opportunities) from further, even accelerated, declines in home prices.

If anything, even the more bearish experts have proven far too optimistic regarding the trajectory of housing's declines. In 2010, for example, Macro Markets LLC interviewed economists and consensus indicated that house prices in 2011 would fall only 0.8 percent, a rate that now appears to be wildly too rosy. In 2009, the Mortgage Bankers Association projected a robust recovery by 2011, lifting prices a full 3 percent. In point of fact, small, temporary recoveries in house prices, spurred only by federal incentives, have proved both uninspiring and transitory. Those small, ephemeral bounces have also distorted the overall market, because the incentives tend to simply delay or pull forward planned purchases anyway. For example, the recent $8,000 first-time buyers' credit simply stole purchases from future months, with the overarching trend (down) normalized and reasserted in ensuing months. In April 2011, a rather shocking Case-Shiller report on national prices detailed a 3.3 percent year-over-year decline in prices. As John Carney of CNBC noted, "We've become passé about home price declines. A 3.3 percent year-over-year decline doesn't seem that shocking anymore. But prior to the recent housing crash, such a steep decline was unheard of . . . this is the opposite of a recovery. It's a crash building steam."[20]

Desert Storm

In Nevada a stunning 67 percent of all borrowers are underwater on their homes. Its desert neighbor, Arizona, ranks second with 49 percent underwater. Not only are half of Arizonans underwater, but for one out of five Phoenix area borrowers, the negative equity is so severe that a *doubling* of their home values is required to bring them back to positive equity! In a state with 9.5 percent unemployment, which added just 1,700 jobs in all of 2010, this situation does not argue for recovery in prices. Nor, in fact, do those numbers argue for a sideways churn along the present lows in price. Instead, the situations in Arizona and Nevada argue for far lower prices to achieve anywhere near a clearing price level. Interestingly, of the five worst states for percentages of homes underwater, four are warm-weather ones—Nevada, Arizona, Florida, and California, the exception being Michigan, hobbled by the auto industry. Obviously, I am biased as a lifelong resident of cold-weather Chicago, but it cannot just be coincidence that warm weather dominates this ignoble ranking, can it? What about warm climates creates loose lending? If ever I buy a bank, I will remember to focus on Vermont and Maine!

But getting back to a national view, this problem is clearly not confined to just the Sunbelt. After all, the building boom in Nevada, for example, clearly fed revenues nationally, as firms like Caterpillar in Peoria, Illinois, prospered from the gush of construction in the Southwest. And so, too, the risks of an underwater nation afflict the national (and global) housing crisis. Emblematic of this national trend, Figure 4.6 displays the severity of the rise in past-due mortgages, looking back 40 years.

One final point on the condition of underwater mortgages. A victim of this upside-down loan status has been structural delinquencies in paying dues to homeowners' associations. As America aged and moved West and South, the preponderance of planned communities soared. In 1970, only 2 million Americans lived in communities governed by a homeowners' association. By 2010, that number had skyrocketed to 62 million.[21] As owners in these communities increasingly fall underwater on their homes, they quite rationally (though not ethically) see little incentive to pay their share of association dues, which cover maintenance, insurance, employees, and so on for these planned

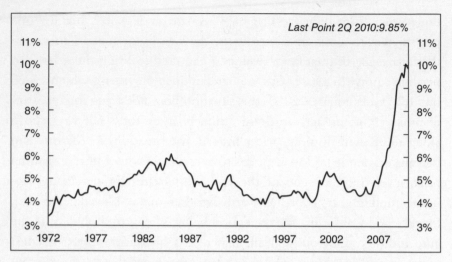

Figure 4.6   Percentage of All Mortgages Past Due (seasonally adjusted)
DATA SOURCE: Mortgage Bankers Association.

neighborhoods. In turn, that delinquency forces many associations to raise dues to bridge the gap from deadbeat residents, which predictably further reduces compliance, and so on. As an example, Rich Vial of Oregon, who runs a law firm representing associations, says his firm's collections cases against owners rose from 632 in 2009 to nearly 3,000 in 2011. And in 2010, Fannie Mae and Freddie Mac announced they would no longer buy mortgages on homes located in associations with delinquency rates above 15 percent, making a local annoyance a truly national issue, with 62 million residents potentially exposed.

If this situation deteriorates, the annual spring square dance night at various Sun City elderly communities might get rancorous!

J. Wellington Wimpy, Borrower

"I will gladly pay you Tuesday for a hamburger today." J. Wellington, commonly known simply as "Wimpy" for decades, has amused *Popeye the Sailor* fans with his dishonest promise to pay later for goods delivered now. But despite Wimpy's eccentricities, his entreaty does in fact form the very basis of capitalism. That is, loans or investment today, the private allocation of capital, in exchange for repayment and profits in the future. Credit remains the fundamental lubrication of the capitalist machine. And a lack of credit, particularly private credit, in the housing markets presents another compelling argument against a housing recovery. Indeed, credit is so tight now that J. Wellington Wimpy would have a hard time getting a hamburger today; even if he could pay 90 percent of the tab, he would likely be denied credit on the remaining balance, and thus forced to either pay cash or do without.

A full four years after the first significant cracks in housing appeared, the private mortgage market remains utterly moribund. In fact, the availability of truly private mortgage credit stands at probably its lowest point since the 1930s. The federal government now guarantees 95 percent of the mortgage market. As I stated earlier in this chapter, the total tab to taxpayers for continued, open-ended funding of the insolvent deferral mortgage agencies already exceeds $100 billion and will likely climb to levels near a half trillion dollars by the time private hands are ready to step back in and lend. For example, the Federal Housing Administration, which requires only 3.5 percent down payment up front for mortgages, accounted for a full 23.5 percent of residential mortgages in 2010. Back in the 1950s, FHA mortgages required 35 percent down. Apparently the taxpayer, thanks to Washington, stands more than willing to repeat the mistakes of Countrywide and Washington Mutual in requiring such a puny down payment for credit! In sharp contrast, overall median down payments were a far higher 22 percent according to Zillow, up from just 4 percent down payment median in 2006 as the mania still persisted. Talk about deleveraging? The private mortgage market has swung the pendulum from "credit-for-all" to "sign over your firstborn and put 30 percent down."

The dramatic shift in lending from private businesses to government enterprises has created a completely flipped reversal in market share in just a few years. At the height of the housing rally, private lenders accounted for 70 percent of mortgage origination, and have now slid all the way to 13 percent. Conversely, government—mainly FHA, Veterans Administration, and Fannie/Freddie—now accounts for 86 percent of originations. And even with the taxpayers assuming this giant burden and becoming lenders on a mass scale, the total market for mortgage originations shrinks significantly. The Mortgage Bankers Association predicts that originations for 2011 will fall to less than $1 trillion in total, down hugely from the already depressed 2010 total of $1.5 trillion, making 2011 the lowest year in total since 1997.[22] A major cause of this severe decline in credit lies in the now stringent demands of lenders. Long gone are the "if you have a pulse, borrow from us" days of easy credit. In its place, the present mortgage market demands very high credentials for credit. For example, the average credit score on loans backed by Fannie Mae rose to 762 in quarter one of 2011 compared to 718 in 2004.[23] Moreover, federal regulators, who de facto control the entire mortgage market now, are proposing very tough new rules requiring originating banks to maintain a stake in loans they securitize and sell if the mortgage borrowers have either low credit scores or down payments below 20 percent. And because there is no effective private secondary mortgage market in operation now, such exclusions would effectively eliminate risky borrowers entirely from mortgages. And given the prevalence of underwater borrowers and high, stubborn joblessness, risky borrowers still abound.

In addition, the lack of credit extends beyond new mortgage origination. Gone too are the go-go days of consumers treating their homes as ATM machines, using low rates to generate "cash out" liquidity. In fact, such refinancing peaked in 2006 at $318 billion total cash withdrawn. In 2010 that figure had shrunk to only $32 billion, as both tighter standards and diminished home equity values have practically eliminated this once-common practice.[24] The Bloomberg Refinance Index, shown in Figure 4.7, shows that, despite historically low rates, the degree of refinances sits near the lows of the range of recent years.

Regarding low rates, Freddie Mac points out that the average 30-year mortgage rate for 2010 was 4.69 percent, the lowest annual rate on record going back to 1972, and yet that incredibly low rate failed

Figure 4.7   The Bloomberg Refinance Index
SOURCE: Bloomberg.

to spur any substantial increase in demand. When the price for a good, any good, declines measurably, and yet demand for that good declines just as fast, or faster, then that market has a lasting, structural problem. In fact most of the buyers lately, particularly of distressed properties, have been all-cash buyers. According to Capital Economics, 70 percent of the increase in the number of new home sales has emanated from cash buyers, while first-time buyers accounted for just 6 percent. Cash buyers represent investors taking a speculative stake, believing the worst is over for housing, and not buyers who want to live in the home. As such, the all-cash crowd represents hot money taking a flier, and that group of buyers would quickly flee when (if) prices take another serious leg lower. In addition, the prevalence of cash buyers verifies the lack of credit for more stable, longer-term would-be buyers. The cost of money keeps falling and yet few seem willing to buy debt, even at depressed prices. Such psychology argues strongly against those who believe in inflationary problems. And that mentality also argues against a housing recovery for many years ahead. The herd, I believe, has become incredibly complacent regarding housing, with wide acceptance of the notion that "it cannot get much worse." It, of course, can—and I believe it will.

"Don't Get High on Your Own Supply"

In the movie *Scarface* about the Miami drug underworld, a ravishing Michelle Pfeiffer plays Elvira Hancock, girlfriend and then wife of drug gangster Tony Montana. One of her memorable lines was advising drug dealers to "never get high on your own supply." In Tony Montana's world, the supply of illicit drugs was far too low for demand, creating giant profits for criminals. Housing has the opposite problem, a supply that totally exceeds any reasonable demand. And a harsh reality of the hangover from the epic housing bender into 2007 is a lingering, enormous supply that will take many more years to work through and achieve any semblance of a return to the price levels that dominated the boom years.

There is much debate about the real supply of houses, either unsold new ones or existing homes for sale. Much of that debate centers on the extent of shadow inventory, meaning houses that need to be sold but have yet to be officially placed on the market, mostly due, ironically, to the poor conditions of the housing sales market. But starting with what is certain, we know that, according to the Census Bureau and the National Association of Realtors, as of Summer 2011, about 4 million homes are officially on the market. See Figure 4.8.

After hitting the totally unsustainable level of 5 million as housing collapsed and nothing sold for a period of months, the good news is that supply has come down to 4 million. The bad news, and it might be much worse than this chart indicates, is twofold: First, the supply is still very far above historical trend, which is more like 2 million homes in inventory. And second, this 4 million home number might seriously understate the actual total inventory. In fact, take a look at Figure 4.9.

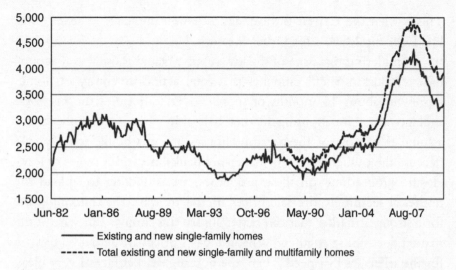

Figure 4.8 Home Inventories (thousands of units, seasonally adjusted)
SOURCE: A. Gary Shilling, *The Age of Deleveraging* (Hoboken, NJ: John Wiley & Sons, 2011).
Reprinted with permission of John Wiley and Sons, Inc.

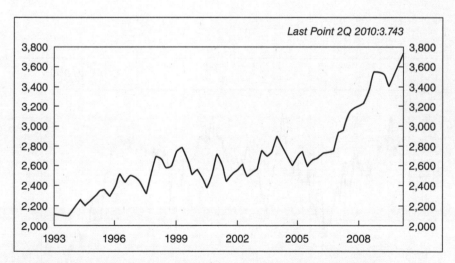

Figure 4.9 Vacant Units Held Off the Market for Other Reasons
SOURCE: U.S. Census Bureau.

This is what the Census Bureau, almost comically, calls "Vacant Units Held Off the Market for Other Reasons."

Considering this issue of shadow supply, David Rosenberg, economist at Gluskin Sheff, estimates that total actual inventory of homes represents about 16 months of supply, over four times the historical average when the housing market is healthy.[25] It is certainly fair to assume that most of these vacant houses are not being actively sold because the owners, many of which are banks in various stages of foreclosure proceedings on these properties, are unwilling to unload the homes at seemingly fire-sale prices. Better to wait, the thinking goes, for a stronger market that can better absorb this supply. But what if the market does not strengthen? What if today's prices are actually a bargain for the sellers, as I suspect? Then, the housing market faces a very bleak future of incredibly bloated supply and a depleted pool of willing buyers too. As Figure 4.10 shows, according to the National Association of Home Builders, the traffic of prospective buyers of new homes con-

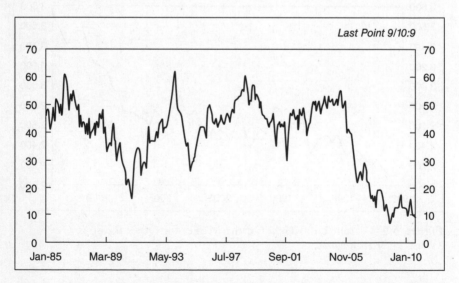

Figure 4.10 Traffic of Prospective Buyers of New Homes (all good = 100)
SOURCE: National Association of Home Builders.

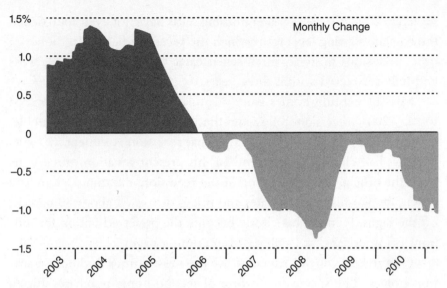

Figure 4.11 Declining Housing Values
SOURCE: Zillow.com.

tinues to trend dangerously downward, as millions of Americans, by choice or circumstances, simply remove themselves from the pool of potential home ownership.

As long as I am frightening you with charts, take a look at Figure 4.11 from Zillow.com, which shows housing values declining for an astounding 57 consecutive months. It is no wonder that sellers fear putting the for-sale shingle out front, and the traffic of buyers recedes heartily.

At the root of this supply issue is foreclosures, both completed and in process. In fact, already some 5 million homes have been foreclosed upon since the crisis began. And Moody's Analytics chief economist Mark Zandi estimates that another 3 to 4 million homes will be foreclosed upon in the next three to four years.[26] Given this incredible weight of supply anchoring down the housing market, it is not surprising that the recovery from this recession, in terms of housing, pales badly in comparison to any previous post-WW2 recession and recovery. For instance, in terms of housing starts, since this recession officially started in 2008, three years later housing starts have not even approached the baseline starting level from which the recession began. In the seven other recessions postwar, in all seven cases the pace of housing starts had fully recovered within three years.

Sales of existing homes paint a similarly dour picture. Compared to the 2001 recession following the bursting of the tech bubble, exacerbated by 9/11, three years after that recession commenced, existing sales had climbed 30 percent. In this present situation, three years from the official 2008 beginning of the recession, existing sales are still down, despite historic low rates and prices depressed about 30 percent off the highs. Renting has clearly become the preferred option for millions of Americans, as I will detail in coming pages.

One area in which I expect to see the most serious declines is vacation homes. The speculative nature of second home purchases during the boom made the degree of leverage on first homes actually seem frugal. In 2006, according to the National Association of Realtors, 1.7 million units sold. By 2008 that number was cut in half. The drop continued, however, with only 543,000 selling in 2010 and 2011 staying on pace for a still lower number. And the median price fell an incredible 11 percent year-over-year from 2009 to 2011. A second home forms the definition of a discretionary purchase. As such, the future for that kind of excess, given the tightness of credit and massive supply, looks bleak indeed. Moreover, resort areas tend to be overly dependent on real estate as a lynchpin of the local economy. For example Vail, Colorado, employed 30,000 people at the highs in 2008. But by 2010, total employment had declined 20 percent, largely because housing employment declined 46 percent.[27]

Form Follows Function

The famed architect Louis Sullivan, one of the earliest purveyors of the modern skyscraper, coined the phrase "form follows function," meaning that the design and shape of a structure should be dictated by its actual use. His strictly utilitarian philosophy of architecture inspired his now more-famous protégé, Frank Lloyd Wright, who popularized a similar-thinking phrase, "less is more." Well, when it comes to another type of architecture, the American home in 2011, many are heeding the wisdom of these bygone architectural greats and deciding that the form, meaning the formation of households, will indeed follow function. That is, consumers, as a key example of the deleveraging process, are forming households at a far lower rate than the recent trend. And this lower rate of household formation argues strongly for yet further declines in housing ahead.

At present the rate of annual household formation has declined to about 600,000, from over 1 million annually at the peak of the building boom.[28] Even more ominously, household formation for the three years ending in March 2010 was about 2.3 million short of the long-term average.[29] Part of the reason is unavoidable demographics. As we discussed in the China chapter, the United States is the only industrial country with projected population growth far into the future. A combination of a comparatively high birthrate and significant immigration has kept the trend upward and will into the future. But even in the United States, the rate of growth is slowing and will slow even more in coming years. The first Baby Boomers turned 65 years old this year, 2011. That giant demographic bulge, now starting to become senior citizens and largely leaving the age of reproduction, will force a slowdown in population growth. In fact, according to the Census Bureau, from 2030 to 2050, the U.S. population will grow more slowly than ever before in its history. And even in the present day, a slower rate of growth is deterring a big natural uptick in household formation.

But most of the near-term slowdown in household formation clearly results from economic, not demographic, influences, all of them negative. To be specific, with the American population right now growing at 1 percent, or about 3 million people per year, and approximately three people per household, one might well expect a rate of one million new households. But the actual 600,000 figure, far lower, signals that deep-seated risk aversion has taken hold. Recent college graduates, for example, facing a brutal job market, live in the bedrooms of their child-hood rather than some cool loft in a trendy part of town, since they are probably unemployed or severely underemployed. Imagine the 24-year-old young man, fresh out of college, degree in hand, working as a Starbucks barista and sleeping on the lower level of a bunk bed he shares with his tweener little brother. This scenario might not impress the 24-year-old's ladies, but the realities of life seem to be dictating just such arrangements, and on a wide scale. According to research of the advertising firm Ogilvy & Mather, about 20 million adult children presently live with their parents. In addition, people are also refraining from divorce. Tough times appear to compel people to stay in seem-ingly tough relationships. Though the divorce rate has been steadily declining for decades, the divorce rate decline hastened with the eco-nomic slowdown. The divorce rate in 2006 was 7.4 per 1,000 people pre-crisis and fell to 6.8 per 1,000 in 2009, according to the National Center for Health Statistics.[30]

If You Build It, They Will Come

Instead of a Field of Dreams in Iowa, as in the Kevin Costner movie, I am referring here to the construction business and Mexican immigra-tion. Another pivotal aspect of lower households rests in far lower immigration, especially illegal immigration. Migrants from Mexico have historically been closely tied to the building trades. And since building was most exuberant in the southwest, near the Mexican border, the 2003 to 2006 housing boom created a particularly magnetic impact on Mexican immigration, both legal and illegal. In turn, those workers helped themselves to soak up housing capacity, albeit generally at the lower end. Still, the response of illegal immigration to economic circumstances is amazingly immediate and rational. People will take great risks to find a good paying job at the end of an arduous journey, but that willingness depletes very dynamically when those opportu-nities dissipate.

As such, a dearth of illegal immigration represents not a proud achievement for America, but rather a foreboding verdict on the struggles facing our housing and employment markets. The Pew Hispanic Center estimates that in 2005 653,000 Mexicans entered the United States, pre-crisis. That figure plummeted to only 175,000 in 2009, and still appears headed even lower.[31] This lack of entry sends two dire messages. First, the Mexicans are staying home because our labor market does not need more workers. And second, the slowdown in immigration will further imperil the serious decline in household formation.

Rent

The 1993 musical *Rent* examined the loves and travails of a group of bohemian artists living in the Lower East Side of Manhattan, struggling to pay rent. For decades, rent has been a price paid by people regarded as inhabiting the margins of society. For example, young people just getting started in careers, or poor people unable to compile the funds for a down payment, or unattached types who move frequently. In contrast, home ownership has been almost lionized, sold by the media and the government as a status symbol, representing stability, financial success, and sharing in the vested interests of communities. Along with a nice car, 2.2 children, and a golden retriever, home ownership has long comprised part of the American vision of achievement. But does owning make sense, at least on the scale that our economy has realized? And regardless of the answer to that question, should the government continue to incentivize home ownership? And finally, given the sharp backup in housing prices, does owning a home make sense?

In the early 1920s, when Herbert Hoover served as Commerce Secretary for President Warren Harding, he declared that "it is mainly through the hope of enjoying the ownership of a home that the latent energy of any citizenry is called forth."[32] How sadly ironic, then, that when President at the beginning of the Great Depression, the countless homeless people who suffered in the dreadful living conditions of ramshackle shanty towns called these pseudo-neighborhoods "Hoovervilles." Similarly, the impoverished masses referred to newspapers as "Hoover blankets." Clearly the whole Depression was not President Hoover's fault, although he provided a very convenient target. And his pronouncements years earlier about housing reflected a long-standing, misguided federal government bias toward home ownership for all.

As America emerged from the Great Depression, the rate of home ownership did recover, hitting about 40 percent by 1940. Then, with the aggressive support of the federal government for decades, the rate steadily climbed to a peak of 69.2 percent in mid-2004. Figure 4.12 shows the last quarter-century of home ownership rates.

Note that until the mid-1990s, the rate flatlined in the mid-60 percents. Then, a combination of the tech boom, federal policy (especially the previously discussed Community Reinvestment Act), and mass mortgage securitization spurred a sharp rise before the descent of

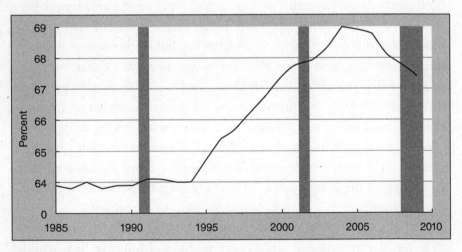

Figure 4.12 Home Ownership Rate for the United States
NOTE: Shaded areas indicate U.S. recessions.
SOURCE: U.S. Department of Commerce, Census Bureau.

the most recent years began in earnest. A 1 percent move in this rate is giant because of the scale involved. America has 112 million house-holds, presently divided between 75 million owners and 37 million renters. So adding 1 percent to the ownership pool translates into another 1.12 million dwellings.[33] Demand for a million new dwellings would do wonders to cure the supply overhang we discussed in recent pages. But I do not at all foresee an increase in this rate. In fact, all trends point to a reversion to mean decline, meaning that the rate of ownership probably needs to decline all the way back to the historical averages nearer 64 percent.

One reason I predict a further decline is the lack of enthusiasm for owning among young people. Among ages 18 and 35, just 38 percent now own a home, down from a peak of 43 percent in 2005. So while the overall rate has fallen about 5 percent, the rate among the young has fallen about double that, or 10 percent.[34] As my friend and noted market maven Dennis Gartman observed: "Those 35 and younger have now been raised in an environment where all they know is that housing prices fall, not rise. Their history is one of buying a $250,000 house and seeing its value fall to $225,000 several years later."[35] For young people today, having been burned in housing (and stocks), the propensity to take risk in home buying is likely minimal, and likely to remain as such for many years ahead, if not forever. This reality is similar to the now very elderly grandparents who lived through the Great Depression and maintained frugal, risk-averse practices for life, having witnessed the wealth destruction of market volatility and broad deflation.

Homes Are Not Investments

The purpose of a home is to provide a roof over one's head that prevents rain from splashing you in the face. Homes are also useful for storage, work, play, protection from vermin (human or animal), and aesthetic beauty. But homes are not investments, and should not be regarded as such. The simple fact is that, adjusted for inflation, homes have been a breakeven investment for a century. One of the key factors depressing true return on investment for homes is ongoing maintenance costs. The average homeowner spends about 3 percent of its value each year on repairs and maintenance, a not inconsiderable sum factored over many years. Combined with insurance, closing costs, and property taxes, the actual "carry" fees of homes mount quickly. Add in some inflation (not that I see inflation as a big issue in coming years) plus hefty broker commissions to sell and, over the long haul, houses have actually made poor investment vehicles. Joseph Gyourko of the University of Pennsylvania Zell/Lurie Real Estate Center, makes this point, detailing that housing prices have, adjusted for inflation, returned 1 percent per year since 1975, without counting the maintenance costs. In contrast, the Moody's Index of corporate bonds rose 6 percent annually in that period, inflation-adjusted.[36] He said "the financial gain of owning a home is likely to be modest . . . there are lots of better ways to accumulate the same amount of expected wealth that do not start off with a 6 percent fee to the broker."

Downward Dog

In yoga, which I have admittedly never tried, one of the foundational exercises is the downward dog stretch. Like much of yoga, downward dog is directed at achieving greater flexibility and thereby strength and injury prevention. Flexibility is indeed crucial in exercise and in life at large. One of the key advantages renting holds over owning is the flexibility and mobility inherent to renting. For example, cities with the highest percentages of home ownership comprise, perhaps counterintuitively, some of the most depressed and least vibrant places in America. For example, in places like Detroit, St. Louis, and Pittsburgh, home ownership percentages exceed the national average, residing up near 75 percent. Detroit is a prime example, with far lower wages and business activity than most American cities. Far too many homeowners feel trapped in those cities, living in homes they cannot sell for any acceptable price, and therefore unable to literally move on and find better opportunities elsewhere. Conversely, cities with low percentages of home ownership, below 60 percent, like New York, Los Angeles, and San Francisco, have higher incomes and far more vibrant, creative economies.

This issue of flexibility has become acutely important in the recent downturn. Certain regions of the country, for example Texas and North Dakota, have thrived, largely because of the energy boom, a combination of high crude oil prices and vast new natural gas flows from horizontal drillings. And jobs abound in both places. But unlike in previous recessions, so far the migration of workers within America has been slow, with few leaving the weak areas seeking jobs in the strong. The hidden reason is largely the housing scenarios millions face: With negative equity, rather than moving, far too many homeowners are sitting in underwater homes, with fingers crossed, and either unemployed or underemployed, with options limited by their house! Further, consider the intangible costs, the anxiety and worry over indebtedness and negative or little equity. Bloomberg recently profiled a young professional in Fair Oaks, California, who rents in a community where property prices plummeted 57 percent off the 2005 peak. Though the prices tempt her to buy, Victoria Pauli ultimately decided to rent again, saying, "I know people who have watched their home value get cut in half . . . it's part of the American dream to own your own home, and I used to feel that way, but now tell myself, be careful what you wish for."[37] Far less fortunate are John and Mary Arrison of Arizona, who bought a house in 2006 for $193,000. They owe $170,000 on their first mortgage and an additional $60,000 on a home equity line. They have stopped paying their mortgage and are now hoping to sell the home via a short sale for $56,000. And the costs extend beyond the financial: "It was a nice street when the Arrisons and their two little boys moved in. Not today, they say. The police have become frequent visitors, drawn by a spate of domestic disputes. A renter nearby scared them with a pair of pet pit bulls."[38]

Given this morose prognostication for housing, what actions make the most sense for an investor willing to stand against the herd that unanimously calls for a housing recovery? First, from a wealth protection standpoint, anyone trying to sell a home should get aggressive on price. In my view, new lows are inevitable given all the serious roadblocks I have outlined in this chapter. Second, for anyone in transition, either moving or renting and considering buying, I recommend patience in buying a home, as I see an even better buyer's market unfolding soon. If I am correct about the deleveraging and concomitant deflationary forces dominating the years ahead, then expect houses to eventually sell for far closer to 10 times one year's rent, rather than to the 20 times multiple seen at the highs. I also see tremendous opportunity betting against companies highly exposed to the building business, especially heavy construction equipment and materials. Lumber, for example, is trading at multi-year lows, and I would willingly sell short into rallies in wood.

On the positive side, a continued decline in home ownership, and home prices, should augment multi-family housing and related businesses as more people rent, either by their own choice, or perhaps with some help from the bank that holds their upside-down mortgage. This trend toward multi-unit rentals should also propel a movement toward generally more dense, more urban living. Much of the recent explosion in the exurbia region, the far outskirt suburbs that boomed in recent years, resulted from easy credit fueling a McMansion craze that should now seriously reverse. Instead of a McMansion 40 miles from the city center and two large SUVs in the garage, I foresee a smaller rental much nearer the city center and public transportation with one car only.

Another less obvious opportunity from the "House of Pain" theme I project is in currencies. As bearishly as I lean regarding the U.S. housing situation, many other countries face, in fact, a far worse exposure to further property declines. Spain, for example, has as many unsold homes as America even though it is one-sixth the size of the United States. Property bubbles in places like Dubai and Shanghai represent far more danger now than the American real estate sphere. As such, I continue to believe that the much-maligned U.S. dollar will begin a multiyear rally, catching global capital offside, far too exposed to the emerging market world, and not nearly enough invested in the United States. With careful, skeptical, independent thought, the maverick investor can avoid the "House of Pain" and perhaps even turn the process into a house of profit.

Chapter 5

You Can't Handle the Truth, or the Volatility

Don't Own Stocks (or at Least Not So Many)

In the movie *A Few Good Men*, Jack Nicholson gave a masterful performance as Colonel Jessup, a fearless, charismatic, if megalo-maniacal, United States Marine officer running the Guantanamo Bay Naval Base. In perhaps the most memorable scene of the excellent film, Tom Cruise's Lieutenant Daniel Kaffee character cross-examines the imposing Colonel on the stand in court-martial proceedings.

"I want the truth!" shouts Kaffee.

"You can't handle the truth!" Jessup famously replies.

To some degree investors share Kaffee's predicament. We really cannot fully handle the truth, of what long-term equity ownership really entails. More to the point, we cannot handle the volatility that is endemic to equities. As such, most investors would do well to resist

Wall Street's conventional wisdom about asset allocation blend. In fact, a 60/40 percent split among equities and bonds is completely inappropriate for most investors, though it sure serves Wall Street very well. The independent-minded maverick investor, however, will constantly question conventional wisdom and, perpetually, critique the actual motivations of advice dispensers and the marketing machines of brokers and asset managers. Once they do so critically and dispassionately, I am confident they will arrive at the conclusion that equities are dangerous for most investors and that the masses would do well to return to the bond-heavy investing styles more familiar to our grandparents than to the equity-heavy culture prevalent since the 1980s.

A Good Walk Spoiled

In 1996 John Feinstein wrote a national bestseller, *A Good Walk Spoiled,* which chronicled the pressure, humor, and eccentricities of professional golf. That phrase, "a good walk spoiled," is used to describe the game of golf and is often attributed to Mark Twain. Well, in the investing world, volatility presents the ever-lurking spoiler of what should be a good walk: saving and investing. Consider the recent wrenching volatility investors have lived through, just since the 1990s. Although investors did endure two very major scares in the autumn of 1997 and 1998 with the Asian and LTCM crises, for the most part the 1990s saw incredible, and almost predictable price advances. The S&P 500 really took off higher in 1994, as the technology revolution took hold with first-time widespread Internet adoption, and the index more than tripled into the millennium turn at the year 2000. Into the Y2K scare, as global governments and companies scrambled to avoid "conversion" problems in all types of systems and technologies, a powerful, combustible combination of heavy tech spending and seemingly endless Federal Reserve liquidity pushed the rally into overdrive.

I was just beginning to work as an independent trader, primarily speculating on the Treasury yield curve. But, like many traders (and far too many nontraders), the allure of equity volatility proved irresistible. So I began trading equity markets in 1999. By the year 2000, I had developed trading models for equities similar to those I had previously run on fixed income markets. In fact, by early 2000, I was largely ignoring bonds and focusing on stocks. On April 4, 2000, I shorted the CME's Nasdaq futures index pre-market before the official opening. I covered later that same day for a 400-point profit. The total range on the day was over 500 points, from above 4200 to below 3700. So my trade captured a 10 percent move *in a single day*. While it was exciting and very profitable for a young upstart trader, it also seared in my mind the enormous volatility possible in stocks. If you have ever read, or ever believed, efficient market theorists, throw such notions out the window. On April 4, 2000, almost no new news hit the market. Instead, a cascade of selling simply fed on itself, as a leveraged, long base run for the exits at once, spurring a mini crash. As remarkably, just one week later, the Nasdaq futures printed almost 4400, recovering an amazing 18 percent off those April 4 lows, before then resuming the violent descent from which is has *still* in 2011 not recovered.

More recently, the housing crash and credit crunch have produced volatility that, at least for nontechnology stocks, has been even more violent. After the autumn of 2002, the S&P 500 commenced an epic rally, nearly doubling in the five years until the fall of 2007. Then, as the housing crisis began to unfold, the S&P 500 melted down from a 2007 high of 1576 to the March 2009 infamous "devil's low" of 666 points, a peak-to-valley decline of almost 60 percent. The rally back upwards, into 2011, has been almost as violent and many, including me, see the serious potential for a major new S&P decline to at least test levels below 1000 again. But the larger point, at least for the purposes of this chapter, is that the volatility of equities has been just immense, and there is no significant reason to expect it will diminish. Is an asset class this volatile appropriate for most investors? The answer is clearly "no," at least not for anyone except very sophisticated, wealthy, and truly long-term holders. From the time I started trading stocks in 1999 to the present, the total price appreciation in the market, in 13 years of investing, has been—zero! We are trading the same S&P 500 prices now in the summer of 2011 as in the summer of 1999 when I began.

Such a long stretch of zero price improvement is not at all unprecedented. For example, the 1970s also represented a similar lost decade. The Dow Jones Industrial Average first touched the then-mythical 1000 point mark in January 1966, before promptly retreating 26 percent into October of that same year. Incredibly, throughout the rest of the 1960s and all of the 1970s, the Dow failed on many attempts to hold value above 1000. The market did not, in any material fashion, truly and lastingly eclipse 1000 until 1983! And for much of that 16-year period, holding equities meant not just a sideways, breakeven proposition, but in fact a losing one, because raging inflation of the 1970s eroded the value of capital that simply treaded water. In fact, in inflation adjusted terms, from November 1968 to July 1982, when Federal Reserve Chairman Paul Volcker finally broke the back of inflation, the S&P 500 actually declined a stunning 64 percent in real terms. Perhaps even more ominously, had you been unlucky enough to buy the market in August 1929 as the Dow Jones Industrial Average hit 386, you did not then realize any profits until 1954. Now that, my friends, means taking buy-and-hold as religious dogma. For any investor of any age, 25 years to break even represents a very long-term time horizon, and it would test the patience of the Biblical character Job. As if these long periods of stagnation were not enough, even timing the good runs has proven incredibly difficult for all but the best traders. In the coming pages, I will warn about just how fierce and heady the competition is in speculating shares, even for smart professionals, much less for part-time traders or hobby investors. But one nugget first, to prove my point: From 1926 to 1996, a literal lifetime, almost all the gain in stocks occurred in only 60 months. So out of 840 total months, the gains were realized in only 7 percent of the total time. Miss more than a few of those months, and even the longest-term gains diminished greatly.

I detail this history of market volatility to argue that the simplistic notion of buy-and-hold for the long term may suit very well the objectives of the brokerage community, mutual funds, and the financial media, but in fact may be a dangerous and frustrating actual strategy for most investors. The truth, in reality, is that most of us can't handle the truth. Just as Colonel Jessup, in his full Marine dress uniform, lectured the cocksure young Lieutenant Kaffee that he could not handle the truth, so too does the roller coaster history of the stock market teach the unemotional student of markets that he (or she) can't handle the volatility. Bogies on the golf course, while meddlesome, really matter little in the game of life, unless you are a professional golfer. But volatility in investing truly does ruin what should otherwise be a good walk.

"Losing Is a Disease"

In the 1984 baseball movie *The Natural*, a psychologist tries to trick the Knights team into winning, declaring in a clubhouse speech that "losing is a disease, as contagious as polio, as contagious as the bubonic plague, but curable." It is true that the mind can work in seriously destructive ways and create losing habits. Indeed, human nature seems more easily geared to such destructive, losing habits than to the disciplines required to win consistently—or at least, *not* lose.

For investors, all but the most steel-nerved individuals will likely find that psychology works powerfully against winning in the market, especially if one accepts the conventional wisdom of buy-and-hold. People first invest in stocks precisely because they believe. They might believe specifically in that company or product or more broadly believe in the general economic vitality. They might believe the advice of a trusted broker or accountant or they might even believe the offhanded tip they overheard at the corner saloon. Whatever the basis, the important premise is that the equity buyer *believes*. As evidence, simply peruse financial websites on the Internet, watch financial television, and talk to investment professionals. Rarely found are serious, professional skeptics. Even rarer are voices telling investors to avoid the asset class of shares entirely. I purport that there exist two powerful reasons, both within the minds of investors, why most people should completely avoid stocks. The first is the tendency to exaggerate the elation and pain of market highs and lows, and the second is the angst and anxiety inflicted upon investors, even in relatively good times.

For example, harkening back to some of the above-cited examples of either violent volatility or drawn-out, lost decades of market returns, every investor needs to ask himself serious, honest questions. For starters, are you truly a long-term investor? That is, will you possibly need this money within 10 years? If so, then absolutely forget about stocks, as the volatility is simply far too risky. Is your time horizon truly 25 years? Then stocks might have a small place in the portfolio mix you construct, but be mindful that if you were unfortunate enough to buy in August of 1929, 20 full years later in 1949 you had still lost more than half your capital, and 20 years is a very long time in anyone's book. During those 20 years, American technology progressed from primitive slow cars to the atomic age, and yet stocks languished. Clearly, I am cherry-picking an awful example, but a nonprofessional investor is at least as likely to invest in shares with great misfortune as to coincidentally pick lows.

Next, all investors need to honestly determine if they can persevere through the painful down moves. For example, those investors who committed capital in 1998, at around the S&P 500 1300-point level, presently stand roughly even on their stock allocation into summer, 2011. But—and this point is key—were they able to hold on that whole time, just to get back to even? Or, unable to take the serious pain of the year 2002, did they hit the eject button at S&P priced at 800? Or, did they sell that infamous post-Lehman demise 666 "devil's low"? And perhaps even more dangerously, did they sell those moments of violent market pain and then, seeing the subsequent intense rallies back, buy back in at much higher prices?

For many, probably for most, investors who fancy themselves long-term buy-and-hold owners of shares, the last decade has resembled a seesaw of selling lows and buying highs. Human psychology almost demands such behavior—that is, getting out of the way of pain and celebrating with the herd during the good times. While such behavior likely has propagated our human species throughout evolution, such a whipsaw of emotions makes for very dangerous and costly investing. Indeed, the maverick, independent-minded contrarian investor rejects the premise of buy-and-hold for stocks. Further, he or she recognizes the limits of human psychology to stick to a plan and act in truly long-term fashion.

The second psychological reason that most investors should avoid shares emanates from the undue stress and mental fatigue involved in dealing with volatility. Few folks prove able to just ignore brokerage statements or checking online balances. In fact, I am regularly amazed at just how real-time and incessantly most professional people of means check—and alter—their portfolios. I once stopped going to a dentist who seemed far more interested in his mobile phone trading platform and Bloomberg Television than caring for my mouth. A friend of mine, a successful New York law partner, was reprimanded by his colleagues who learned, though an office-wide computer system audit, just how much work time he was spending trading and researching his online brokerage account. And given how involved most people become in their portfolios, the stress inflicted during bad times can grow into a real impediment to all sorts of life's pursuits, from performing well professionally to interacting pleasantly and patiently with children. Those of us who trade full-time for a living still find it difficult to compartmentalize market stress, particularly given the 24-7 nature of global markets at present. If a professional person, say a realtor or professor, adds to her normal career stress the additional stresses of serious market risk—meaning the loss of principal—then she will undoubtedly find it more difficult to manage a myriad of life's other obligations.

The potential loss of principal represents perhaps the strongest reason of all to avoid too much exposure to stocks. For some people, the truly wealthy, serious equity allocation might make sense, assuming they can avoid or manage the stress of principal losses. Someone with a $100 million net worth, even at recent lows of market swings, down over 50 percent, might not have been forced to make real lifestyle changes. The wealthy CEO's son still attended Princeton and drove an expensive car, regardless of the S&P's volatility. But to a person with a $1 million portfolio, intending to save for education, retirement, and unexpected expenses, losing 50 percent of its value at the lows probably triggered very real and unpleasant lifestyle decisions, particularly if combined with a serious loss of equity (or principal) on a home.

That point about home equity is crucial too. In the early 1980s, the average mortgage holder had about 50 percent equity in the home. By 2010 that equity percentage had fallen all the way to 19 percent. On a macro scale, then, the toxic combination of falling houses and falling stocks inflicted much pain, realized and internal to the mind, upon investors who were, and are still, too exposed to stocks. And sadly for so many investors, Wall Street and its marketing machine have so successfully wooed the masses into the culture of equity ownership that the risks in many ways exceed the risks of the Great Depression era. In 1929, stocks had clearly grown into a national obsession, but in reality, for most people, they remained a spectator sport, as only 3 percent of all Americans owned stocks then.

Coach Bill Belichick and John Maynard Keynes

In 2009, Coach Belichick's New England Patriots played an important late-season game against the Indianapolis Colts, pitting perhaps the two best quarterbacks in the league in a showdown, Tom Brady versus Peyton Manning. With 2:00 left in the game on their own 28 yard line, facing fourth down and two yards to go, Belichick decided to go for the first down rather than punt. New England did not make the yardage, and instead turned the ball over to Manning and crew, who marched into the end zone to come from behind and win. Because Indianapolis had no time-outs left, a first-down conversion would have ended the game with New England taking a couple of knees and marching off the field victorious. But once the decision failed, Belichick endured endless criticism in the sports media for losing the game. Had he, in fact, made the right call, though, regardless of the actual outcome? The answer, statistically, is emphatically yes.

Statistically, as evidenced by many studies from reputed mathematicians, NFL teams should actually never punt on fourth down in opponent's territory, no matter the yardage required on fourth down. And, depending on how far the distance required for a first down, most studies determine that a team should go for the first down all the way back to their own 20 yard line or so. Given that the Patriots faced fourth and 2 at their own 28 yard line, Belichick was clearly correct in going for the conversion, doubly so when considering that a successful attempt would, with certainty, ensure the final outcome. Why then did Belichick take such heated criticism for his move? And why do so few coaches make the statistically correct call and frequently forgo punting on fourth down with advantageous field position?

The answer lies in the false comfort of crowds and crowded thinking. From a human behavioral standpoint, thinking "outside the herd" is considered risky for evolutionary reasons. That is, the logic of primitive safety in numbers dictated that humans, as both predators and prey in nature, seek the safety of multitudes and cooperation. And in the NFL, and football in general, the crowd, which is anything but dispassionate, cares little for the statistical efficacy of an apparently risky decision. Instead, the legions of fans focus far more on field position than the actual odds of scoring (and preventing scores). In addition, they find unacceptably unnerving the near-term fright associated with trying for the first down, forming up at the line of scrimmage, staring down the opposing defense. Instead, most fans, and clearly most sports journalists, would rather take the apparently safer route of a predictable, but actually more risky, punt downfield. Behavioral finance largely replicates this same process. That is, money managers, whether professional or just amateurs, prefer, almost inherently, the safety of the herd. For this reason, very few managers outperform the indexes by any significant, lasting degree. The irony is that, in markets, as in NFL fourth and short situations, following the herd is actually more dangerous than thinking independently, even if Belichick's bold call did not succeed.

The tough reality is that comfort is rarely rewarded in business in general, or in markets specifically. The thoughtful contrarian, therefore, faces a mentally tough, though far safer, path. Famed British economist John Maynard Keynes spoke to this point when he stated:

It is the long term investor . . . who will in practice come in for [the] most criticism, wherever investment funds are managed by committees or boards or banks. For it is in the essence of his behaviour that he should be eccentric, unconventional and rash in the eyes of average opinion. If he is successful, that will only confirm the general belief in his rashness; and if in the short run he is unsuccessful, which is very likely, he will not receive much mercy. Worldly wisdom teaches that it is better for reputation to fail conventionally than to succeed unconventionally.[1]

I am surely no Keynesian when it comes to matters of government interference in the economy, but Lord Keynes hit a 400-foot home run in his assessment of human psychology and the mental requirements to add real "alpha" or market return not simply generated from sticking to index moves. Belichick, as he makes clear to the world in his almost unbelievably slovenly sideline attire, cares little for reputation and instead concentrates on results. Thus, he fears little the risk involved in failing unconventionally. In that regard, Belichick resembles another maverick thinker we've profiled in this book, Dr. Michael Burry, who saw earlier than almost anyone the insane risks endemic to the subprime mortgage markets. And, like Belichick, even in spite of his clear successes, Burry endured unfounded criticisms. Amazingly, Burry ended up closing his fund and managing only his own money as he found himself unable to deal with the irrational demands of his investors, despite reaping them serious fortunes through his unconventional practices. As an example of how irrational and herd-following the investing crowd can be, consider that Burry manages no investor money, despite his incredible, creative genius. Yet, in contrast, the America Funds' "Growth Fund of America" managed an incredible $140 billion at the end of 2010, despite a 10-year net-of-fees return of under 3.5 percent and a 2007 to 2009 peak-to-valley descent of over 40 percent. That contrast alone proves Lord Keynes right.

The herd instinct is not confined to only the actual investors, whether pros or amateurs, but also to the research community. Admittedly, circumstances have certainly improved regarding sell-wide research from the Wall Street brokers, meaning they are more honestly analyzing companies rather than making boilerplate recommendations that every company should be bought. Most of these companies, not coincidentally, bring important fees themselves to the firms. But even still, after the scandals of tainted analysts and an incredible $1.4 billion in total fines, "sell" ratings on stocks are still far too rare.

Better Have Strong Hands

One of the more humorous traditions in professional sports is the training camp hazing of rookies. Most players who can earn a tryout spot succeeded mightily at the collegiate level, and probably enter the NFL scene with little experience in being humiliated, especially on the football field. But as part of long-standing NFL ritual, the rookies endure countless minor humiliations that range from head shaving to being taped to goalposts to dressing up in costume for team travel. Perhaps the most common, though, is that rookies are responsible for carrying all the equipment off the field for the veterans. Luckily, anyone seeking an NFL career has very strong hands.

Similarly, anyone seeking to trade markets seriously needs to have very strong skills and determination. Despite my criticisms of most money managers and most Wall Street research, the simple fact remains that markets are dominated by a relatively small, incredibly well capitalized, technologically advanced, and very skilled group of traders and hedge funds. The bad news for regular investors, even those who pay close attention to markets, is that your competition is incredible and their skill and other advantages render you unlikely to achieve serious profits, at least without taking outsized risks.

First, recognize that the competition is ruthless because the stakes are so high. The list of richest Americans is increasingly dominated by billionaire hedge fund managers. Because succeeding in markets brings such outlandish rewards compared to, say, succeeding in accountancy, the level of competition naturally elevates massively. Because this competition is so intense and dominated by such skilled players, the opportunity to find "bargains" becomes nearly impossible. Too many smart people, with too much technology and better information, have already closed those mispricings. Notice, I am not advocating the efficient market theory. As I mentioned earlier, I believe markets can, and do, act emotionally and inefficiently. But I also believe that an increasingly small group of traders and funds is successfully exploiting those opportunities long before they become apparent to regular investors or even traditional money managers. Further, technology is fast becoming more and more important to the financial markets. I am amazed, when visiting the clients of my research firm, Veracruz, how little trading floors of the best firms resemble the Wall Street of the eponymous 1980s movie. Instead, trading floors increasingly resemble Google, dominated by young mathematicians, engineers, and programming wizards. Why? Because the business of high-speed, algorithmic trading, wherein computers trade according to predetermined strategies, without any human input, increasingly dominates the financial markets. Market analyst James Altucher pointed out this predicament for the regular investor:

I know [a] guy. He has code that scours the FDA databases looking for microscopic changes in any documents. You know what happens when some of those documents change just a little? A press release comes out a week later. A stock gets halted. It opens up or down 50 percent. Who is going to win the dollar? You, or the guy who wrote 100,000 lines of code scouring the FDA databases.[2]

Altucher is right. The game is simply too hard for a non-pro—and sometimes even for the pros! But the advantages of better information, better technology, and speed of programmed trading make it unlikely that the casual investor can achieve true "alpha," or returns above and beyond the expected returns of just buying an index fund.

I never showed up at NFL training camp, even though I so love the game. Why? Because I am simply outmatched and would not even try to compete, knowing the sure painful outcome. Similarly, regular folks should avoid the financially and psychologically bruising competition involved in equity ownership. Instead, the maverick contrarian thinker should recognize the inherent conflicts of interest motivating Wall Street and mutual funds that convince the masses to buy in. And, at least with the vast majority of his capital, that independent thinker should avoid equity exposure, as the risks to the pocketbook and psyche far outstrip the rewards. Moreover, the contrarian, unafraid to step away from the crowded herd, will be far better served focusing on building predictable savings, the way grandma and grandpa did "way back when," and shun the tempting but ultimately dangerous culture of owning shares in companies. Later in this chapter, I will give detailed ideas about how to save safely and profitably in bonds.

At this point you may be asking, "Well, why don't I just invest with the best then?" Two answers there: First, because they won't have you unless you are very wealthy, since most successful funds are closed to new investors or require very high minimums, into many millions of dollars. Second, even the best and brightest stumble badly. For example, in 2008, Warren Buffett, perhaps the greatest investor of all time, lost nearly 50 percent for his investors peak-to-trough. In addition, though he profited in 2009, he badly underperformed the S&P for the whole rally off the lows from March to December 2009.

"Girls Just Wanna Have Fun"

The hit 1983 song by Cyndi Lauper declared that "Girls Just Wanna Have Fun." She extols that, in the face of questioning fathers and societal pressures, in the end, fun was her destination. And indeed girls (and boys) do often simply want to have fun. I am no killjoy, and I readily admit that stock investing can be terrific fun. In fact, one of the reasons I trade for a living is that I find the whole puzzle of markets fascinating and fun. But two caveats:

- First, I do it full time, living and breathing markets around the clock.
- Second, even I do not venture often into the realm of actual individual company stocks, much preferring a more macro approach using Treasury bonds, currencies, commodities like crude oil, and then sector exchange traded funds (ETFs) within the world of equities.

The reason? Even though my network on Wall Street is vast and my experience trading nearing two decades, I still believe I can ascertain no real edge on specific companies. In other words, even a whiz programmer at John Paulson's hedge fund has no empirical advantage over me in forecasting the level of U.S. Treasury interest rates, say, three months from now. Nor does he have an inherent edge in assessing the likelihood of a macro event occurring such as a tax cut by Congress.

But in determining the reaction to the earnings release after-hours of XYZ Widgets Inc? There, the specialists hold significant advantages, and so I rarely choose to play in the sandbox of company shares.

If you're an investor looking to have similar fun in the game of equity investing, my advice is simple: Carry on, but keep it small. Like any other recreation, no one can object as long as the costs—mental and financial—do not far outweigh the excitement of playing. And clearly, just like in Las Vegas, people do occasionally get lucky. It is entirely possible that you can buy into, at very low prices, the next Apple ready to explode and reap profits that can change your life. In the dot-com days I had a once-in-a-lifetime lucky trade in shares, though, perhaps tellingly, it was a short, not a long!

Through friends I came to know a number of the very early employees of Exodus, which became an Internet darling. At one point, as it appeared to rule its segment of the technology world, half of all Internet crossing packets traversed Exodus's network. It grew to 4,500 employees and achieved a staggering peak market capitalization value of $32 billion. Over many talks late into the night with these employees, though, I became convinced that the market was massively overvaluing this company. At its essence, it provided air conditioners for web hosting and data storage. This company was nothing like Cisco or Intel, companies truly forging innovations with high barriers to entry for competitors. So, I shorted the shares and my timing was incredibly lucky. By 2001, Exodus declared bankruptcy and crashed and burned. I stayed short nearly the whole way down, and was fortunate enough to pay for much of my first home with those profits. But, I recognize that score for what it was, a lucky strike. My trade involved no rigor, no discipline, and carried no macro overarching motivation in contrast to, say, my very bearish views on China presented in this book. Nonetheless, the profits were real, and I probably used up my one lucky market score.

Investors seeking some fun in the market should recognize that the likely outcome is losing money. As long as that practice is truly an intellectually and emotionally rewarding endeavor, and as long as the total percentage of your portfolio allocated to fun stays very low, then I say have at it, channel Cyndi Lauper and have fun.

Sadly, in Investing There *Are* Valleys Low Enough

"Ain't No Mountain High Enough" was another iconic song from two greats: Marvin Gay, and later Diana Ross and the Supremes. The song describes how no valley could be deep enough to prevent the singer from reaching his (or her) lover. One of the most pronounced problems with equity investing is that there are indeed valleys so low, meaning the loss of capital, that those valleys make capital recovery an aggressively difficult task. When an investor allocates a healthy portion of his savings to equity ownership, he risks the loss of principal, which is, of course, not only an inherent risk, but in fact at some point highly likely. And then the math starts to work against the investor, no matter what the conventional wisdom of finance prescribes. For example, once an account experiences the 40 percent losses that were typical in 2008, from that valley a total return of 150 percent must be realized just to get back to even. Lose 20 percent, and a 25 percent return is required. Few people realize just how important capital preservation is until a good chunk of capital is lost. They then realize that, unlike the Supremes singing, the valley of capital losses is so low that recouping capital becomes an almost insurmountable task.

After suffering such stinging losses, the willingness (and perhaps even ability) to take serious market risk naturally dissipates, making the recovery process even more arduous. Perhaps investors lucky enough to buy the 2009 S&P 666 low print will never have to worry about going net negative on their accounts. But consider that only a lucky few bought in those volatile, frightening days and held on. And further, even if an investor did put capital to work at S&P 666, they are very likely buying more now at twice that price, and effectively averaging their net entry price much higher. Consider the alternative scenarios. What about the investor who bought into Wall Street's shameless peddling of the tech bubble and paid prices near the top? If one bought in above Nasdaq 100 Index 4800 in March of 2000, here 11 years later, it still requires an astounding doubling of the Nasdaq just to get back to even, after more than a decade! Or consider someone who eschewed technology, perhaps sensing the frothiness of the Silicon Valley obsession and instead bought Ford Motor at that same time, paying about $25 per share. They too require a near doubling just to get back to even.

My point is that losses hurt, not just emotionally and financially in the near term, but in the long term by forcing the math to work against capital recovery. Preservation of capital is simply a hallmark principal, and one far too easily overlooked by the investment management community. But the independent thinker will realize that for the vast majority of her portfolio, solid interest earnings represent the best long-term capital growth strategy. I am confident that in coming years just such investing will become far more the norm, as households deleverage and bring our savings rate far closer to historical norms.

Demographics are at play here too, because the Baby Boomers now moving into retirement really have no choice but to save diligently and safely. They cannot handle another round of intense volatility as they enter the phase of life most attuned to saving. One of the real casualties of our culture of equity ownership has been the previously standard notion of savings. In fact, in 1980, before the equity cult became widely accepted, our savings rate was in double digits even as the bulk of society was young. Then, 18 percent of Americans were in their 20s, an age range not typically commensurate with high savings. In 2010, only 14 percent of Americans were in their 20s, and the savings rate had collapsed over those 30 years. I project that it will slowly but inexorably rise in the coming years until it again catches the unemployment rate, most likely somewhere near 9 and 10 percent for each.

A Very Good Place to Start

In *The Sound of Music*, Governess Maria teaches the Von Trapp children to sing by starting "at the very beginning" with the notes of a song. The beginning is a good place to start with investing too, only the fundamental rule of this world is:

Protect your principal.

As demonstrated in this chapter, volatility in equities is too extreme and hard emotionally to handle. Long-term returns in shares do not justify the risks inherent with equity ownership. And most people have neither the wealth nor the discipline to handle inevitable sharp draw-downs. But most important of all, when investing, is learning not just to win, but how not to lose—not fall into the valley of capital losses, forcing the math to work against recovery.

If you must follow Wall Street's dangerous 60/40 bonds-to-stocks blend, then at least develop a system. Only through a system can one try to avoid the typical investor pitfall of buying jubilantly at highs and selling resignedly at the lows. For those who cannot or will not shake the equity ownership habit, I suggest using the 10/25 model developed by James Stewart, a financial advisor perhaps best known for his columns in the *Wall Street Journal*. He uses the Nasdaq, and I concur thoroughly with using an index, since stock picking is a practice pursued by the masses but mastered by very few. He robotically buys every 10 percent dip in the index and then sells on every 25 percent rally.[3] It is longer term in focus, a sensible way to try to market time for busy nontraders, and has worked very well over time. I clearly prefer that most investors simply avoid that asset class entirely, but if you must dance, Mr. Stewart's approach represents an effective routine for the equity dance floor.

My advice is to build a lifetime of capital appreciation on the foundation of bonds. A mix of Treasuries, corporate bonds, and some municipals makes sense for most investors. Starting with Treasuries, the simple yet incredibly crucial, elemental necessity of Treasury bonds for every portfolio is the fact that they are riskless. That trait of risklessness represents a most underrated attribute, even in spite of the financial tumult of recent years. So strong is the culture of equities in our society, strengthened over 30 years of hard selling, that the public seems unwilling, still, to embrace fixed income adequately.

Let me make a few points about risk here. I am not at all anti-risk. In fact, life, in many ways, presents on ongoing balance between necessary risk and concomitant reward. There is, of course, no free lunch, and any success requires risk. Examples: the risk of asking a girl out who later becomes your wife; the risk of playing violent football to win a scholarship to Stanford; the risk of starting a business; and the risk of writing a book hoping against hope that people will read it! I am an entrepreneur and full-time trader and I live risk every day. But directing and channeling risk presents the key challenge. By that, I mean people should absolutely embrace risk, but only in areas of some proficiency. For example, the established, talented landscaper should absolutely invest in his business, by buying new trucks, advertising, hiring more people, all risk propositions to be sure. But he should not then take his hard-earned landscaping profits and lose serious capital because Europe suffered a currency crisis. Or, for example, a young upstart journalist working at a stable job at an established magazine, who leaves to take an equity stake in a startup digital media company. Again, that risk makes sense and might pay handsomely. But for the writer to watch her 401k diminish because of inflation in China represents an asymmetric risk. She worked too hard to save and then have to watch her capital disappear in something utterly unrelated to her area of proficiency. I trade stocks every single day, but as a Wall Street actor looking from the inside out, when I see the advice and plans sold to the investing public, I want to scream "no . . . think!" Is this plan really in your best interests or that of your broker? Can you really tolerate, financially and emotionally, serious drawdowns of capital in your account? And are you truly in this for the long term, meaning decades, not a few years? I think the honest answer, for most investors, to those questions is "no."

Therefore, Treasuries must constitute a pillar of any portfolio, plus the premise of the "principle of protecting principal." Treasuries, considered staid and boring, have performed remarkably well for over 30 years, ever since the United States kicked the inflation habit of the 1970s. And, if I am even partially right about the disinflationary forces facing the world, I suspect Treasuries still have very bright years ahead. It is crucial to realize, though, that in comparing bonds to stocks, analysts often compare apples and oranges. They often cite low annual returns for bonds, but they are making one of two errors (or both).

First, they're likely citing buying a longer-dates Treasury, say a 20-year bond, and then tracking its return over the whole 20 years. The problem with that approach is that as the bond nears maturity, it no longer behaves as a long-term bond. At year 18, for example, it is a very sideways-moving two-year note, functioning like cash rather than a long bond. The second, related mistake is using the return of bond funds composed totally, or mostly, of very short-term maturities. Once again, such funds tend to act as enhanced savings accounts, with money market returns. I propose, on the other hand, remaining over the years in the long end of the curve, where bonds really act like bonds, providing not just safety, but also solid yield returns. By rolling a long bond, say, every year into another 20- or 30-year instrument, an investor preserves the true long-term Treasury exposure. And doing so, despite the roaring bull market of the 1980s and 1990s in stocks, bond investors handily beat the returns earned by shares, with a fraction of the risk. Gary Shilling points out that after investing $100 in 25-year zero coupon bonds in the year 1981, and rolling it annually as I recommend, the total return by 2010 was $13,532, for an 18.8 percent annual return. In contrast, that same $100 in shares grew to only $2,255 (assuming re-invested dividends). Figure 5.1 shows the sharp, long-term bond outperformance, even in times of raging bull equity moves.

Moreover, many critics of bonds will protest that tying up capital for 30 years for a paltry 4 percent return just doesn't make sense. I advocate, though, that a guaranteed return of principal, plus 4 percent, represents an incredible bargain for the investors, especially compared to shares. For example, the present dividend yield of the S&P 500 is about 2 percent. Promising only a 2 percent yield, and of course no promise at all of return of principal, makes the Treasury market seem highly appealing to me. For many years after the Great Depression, equity yields were actually *higher* than Treasury yields, for this very reason. Because principal was not (and is not) protected, and because investors then saw shares far more as yield than growth plays, shareholders demanded a yield premium above Treasuries. I don't know if we're headed for a return to those kinds of yields again on stocks, but I do

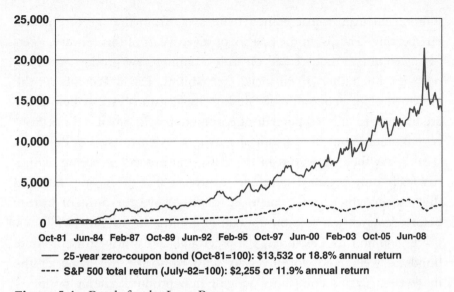

Figure 5.1   Bonds for the Long Run
SOURCE: A. Gary Shilling, *The Age of Deleveraging* (Hoboken, NJ: John Wiley & Sons). Reprinted with permission of John Wiley and Sons, Inc.

believe strongly that equity dividend yields need to rise significantly. Either companies need to start using their massive cash hoards to raise dividends, or the share prices need to decline, thereby inherently lifting the dividend yield, and very likely some combination of the two. I would get far more interested in shares if the S&P 500 dividend yield significantly exceeded the same percent level as the 10-year Treasury. For most investors, especially those of modest means who cannot handle the volatility of corporate bonds, for example, Treasuries should constitute at least half of their portfolio.

Given the macro forces I have detailed in this book—emerging market (EM) risk, especially in China; Japan reeling; housing continuing its descent—the long-term outlook for Treasuries remains outstanding. In a world of deleveraging and benign pricing, Treasuries will shine. They may not provide the thrill of biotech shares, for those who want to check their online account hourly. But for the long-term investor who wants to responsibly protect principal and grow wealth, Treasuries represent a solid stairway to success. Moreover, Treasuries will benefit from a macro movement away from the age of financial engineering. That is, in the first six or seven years of this century, assets advanced not so much based on truly stunning new products or technologies, but rather on financial mechanisms. David Rosenberg, the esteemed chief economist of Gluskin Sheff, estimates that before the credit crunch, fully 40 percent of corporate profits emanated not from core businesses but from financial activities.[4] After trillions of dollars in wealth was then destroyed in the crisis, the process of raising savings has really only begun. I continue to project that the savings rate and the unemployment rate will meet, as they have for most of history before America was sold on the cult of equities in the early 1980s.

In addition to Treasuries, I also certainly see a place for corporate bonds as well. And, for investors who truly like the game of the market—analyzing companies, judging new products, timing cycles—I advise playing in corporate bonds, which have some equity-like characteristics of the underlying company issuing the debt, but are far safer and, I believe, better investments than common stock. First, bonds carry important legal rights absent to equity holders. If a company does get into fiscal straits, bondholders stand first in line at the credit window. Even in bankruptcy, historically bondholders have gotten a large amount of their principal back. Porter Stansberry, of the excellent eponymous advisory service, points out that since 1920 the default rate on the lowest tier of investment grade 10-year bonds (Baa) has been 7 percent. And the recovery rate (meaning the amount of principal that the investor ultimately recoups after a default) for corporate bonds, since 1987, has been 46 percent. So if seven of your 100 corporates default, a reasonable historical assumption, then you would still recover roughly half of that amount, meaning the true default loss, over time, is likely to be only about 3.5 percent. Even for junk bonds, which have a cumulative 5-year default rate of a much higher 21 percent, the recovery rate for bondholders has also been about half, the same as for investment grade bonds.

The main point is that Treasuries, with no risk, and corporate bonds, with acceptable risks, should make up nearly all the portfolio for nearly every investor. First, for reasons of safety and predictable growth, and secondly because the world faces a prolonged period of slow growth and restrained prices. We think little about deflation because only the very oldest people alive can remember it. But global forces, especially the emerging market bubbles, slowing population growth, and global industrial overcapacity are all combining to forge a world without pricing power. Anecdotally, you probably notice it already in certain areas of your life. Can your accountant or lawyer raise her rates on you? Likely not. Would you pay up for a builder to remodel your kitchen right now, knowing how idle most construction related firms are at present? I know I will not buy anything at the major clothing chains until I receive one of the dozen-times-daily coupon offers. And those offers are not for 10 or 15 percent off, but for 40 or 50 percent off. The world lacks pricing power, except for the notable exceptions of food and energy, but I submit those too were not demand-driven but rather Federal Reserve QE policy-driven. That is, Bernanke achieved exactly the wrong result, creating inflation not in wages or housing, as anyone would have hoped, but instead in basic commodities, crushing the middle class with no wiggle room in today's home budgets.

Another macro reason inflation is remaining tame is falling wages due to lower unionization. Workers have to compete globally, and with union membership now down near 10 percent of the workforce, far off the 25 percent typical for many decades, the pricing power of most workers is very tepid.

Unforgettable and Unrepeatable

I surmise many equity bulls feel like Nat King Cole when they consider the stock world before 2008. The 1980s, 1990s, and first years of the twenty-first century were indeed "unforgettable." But I would also argue that they are unrepeatable. One-time macro factors combined to create a kind of bullish perfect storms for shares. Now, all those trends are reversing, changing the unforgettable into unrepeatable, presenting perhaps the most crucial of all reasons to avoid stocks. I would argue that the confluence of macro trends evident in the 25 years between 1982 and 2007 were outliers in history and unlikely to reoccur, certainly not in our lifetimes. Specifically, during this quarter-century period, the cult of equities became an easy sell, because three massive macro factors merged into a powerful foundation for a secular rally. These factors were:

- Demographics
- World peace
- Free market policies

I will lay out how these macro tailwinds propelled equities higher and why they are unlikely to be repeated, at least not anytime soon.

Demographics is destiny in many ways. Throughout this book I have mentioned various demographic forces. I think focusing on demographics illuminates macro opportunities—and risks—because demographic trends can be projected with a fair degree of certainty, and yet these trends are mostly ignored by the investing world. For example, of the legions of China cheerleaders on Wall Street, one would be hard pressed to find someone analyzing the coming decline in Chinese population, especially the young, and the hastening of the Lewis point of exhausting cheap labor. Similarly, I believe long-term investors do not at present sharply differentiate between the United States and Europe, even though the United States population grows while Europe's implodes, especially in places such as Italy and Spain. There are only two ways to grow an economy: Either population or productivity must grow, and preferably both. Given that the United States has both, shouldn't U.S. companies be valued at a far higher premium than Spanish ones? And, for that matter, the same for the U.S. dollar versus the euro.

Alas, I believe Wall Street misses the forests for the trees on these issues and pays far too little heed to the primacy of demographics. In the 25-year golden period for shares, the demographic tailwind blew at gale force behind economies and equity markets. The Baby Boomers were just moving into their peak earnings and savings years, typically when a person enters their 40s. It is hard to overestimate the importance of this trend. A giant wave of people, born in the post-WWII birth boom, raised in a prosperous, growing America, educated better than any other demographic group in human history, hit the peaks of their productivity and earnings years, fueling equities and all manners of assets. The only trouble is—it is over. The boomers did not produce another such boom of babies. While America is growing population far better than our industrial peers, we're still growing population far more slowly than those randy Marines back from Guadalcanal did. As the ratio then changes, we become a nation that produces and consumes less as the boomers age. For example, from the late 1960s to the late 1980s, the percentage of the population aged 20 to 49 versus the percentage over 50 grew steadily, peaking around 1988 just under 1.8 to 1.0. But ever since, that ratio has dwindled, and is starting to accelerate downward, sure to reach 1 to 1 in the 2020s. Again, demographic trends are immutable once entrenched. One of the foundational premises for the boom of the 1980s and 1990s was very favorable demographics as the Boomers soared in productivity, income, and spending. Now, as those Boomers turn to shuffleboard, 4:30 P.M. dinners, and *Matlock* reruns, the whole cult of equities will find a far less robust demographic underpinning.

Secondly, the 25-year equity boom celebrated, quite properly, a time of relative peace in the world. Though myriad regional disputes have persisted in the post-WWII period, the broad theme has been, quite contrary to the preponderance of human history, absence of serious global conflict. Not at all to minimize the human tragedy or conflict that has occurred, but the point is that 60+ years of macro peace are unusual and, again, unlikely to persist forever. In fact, perhaps the greatest danger of the economic dislocations I foresee, especially the emerging market reckoning, will be the temptation of failing governments and people to turn to violence and scapegoating. In addition, the fall of the whole Marxist system unleashed an incredibly powerful collection of forces favoring capital assets. The opening of markets, reduction of defense budgets, and general optimism engendered by the fall of the Berlin Wall created an enormous amount of global wealth.

Going forward, is a similar catalyst on the horizon? It seems not. Communism represented a global threat on several fronts. First, it obviously opposed free markets as a foundational principle. Second, its outward expansionist aggression required serious Western (really American, to be fair) resources to counter. And third, its psychological impact dampened creativity, as a people focused on possible nuclear Armageddon clearly do not innovate at optimal levels. But by the mid-1980s the writing was on the wall, so to speak, that communism was doomed. And once that wall—the Berlin Wall—fell, the 1990s enjoyed an era of peace and prosperity unrivaled in history. But again, a similar catalyst does not appear to be present now. The one-time special dividend of the fall of Marxism as a serious global movement has been spent. Because the world is unlikely to witness such a macro market support in coming years, this void represents yet another reason to avoid equities and expect slow growth in the next decade.

The third macro tailwind is closely related to the fall of Marxism. America, led by Ronald Reagan, successfully exported to the world the idea of free market capitalism. Even the Communist Party of China ceased to be communist in the economic sense (though they remained decidedly so in the political sense). As America won the global battle of ideas regarding economics, markets rightly responded in kind. As markets opened and creativity flourished, global governments receded from interference and unleashed untold innovation and wealth. But if anything, this trend of openness and free markets is already reversing. That reversal should not really surprise us. After all, post-crises, generally the cry for intervention and controls rises again. The masses foolishly believe that more government control might stem the negative impacts of a credit crisis, even though I believe that government fingerprints lie at the very founding base of the crisis! Moreover, once bubbles burst, the natural reversion sends politics on a collision course with markets, as firms and individuals who allegedly caused or profited from the bursting become whipping posts for general anger. In recent days the relentless, baseless attacks on Goldman Sachs represent the worst American example of this anti-business, anti-market sentiment. I also foresee an unmistakable trend developing concerning international trade. The United States's refusal to allow Dubai Ports to purchase port assets in America, for example. Or the implied refusal to allow the Chinese to purchase Unocal. Controls on international mergers and, more importantly, free trade will surely grow ever more onerous. In fact, once China starts to really sputter, one of their only options will be dumping products on the world at bargain basement costs in an attempt to boost cash flow. I project that such deflationary dumping will spur a global trade war, as workers in developed nations will surely cry foul and demand reprisals. Already the pace of trade disputes rises steadily. Such a trend presents an ominous threat to global growth, as global trade as a percentage of world GDP has risen from 18 percent in 1990 to an incredible 26 percent today.[5] As Pulitzer Prize-winning author David Yergen correctly postulates: "The era of easy globalization is over. The power of the state is reasserting itself."[6]

The irony is that free trade has been, on net, a massive creator of jobs, even though it clearly displaces some inefficient workers in America. David Smick, in his excellent book *The World Is Curved*, points out that from NAFTA's enactment in 1993 to 2001, total American employment grew from 120 million to 135 million, and five years into the trade pact, U.S. unemployment hit a historic low of 3.8 percent.[7] A future of less free trade, then, presages less employment, less growth, and therefore less advantage in owning equities. The trend of the 25 years from 1982 to 2007 was openness, trade, and a world increasingly captivated by capitalism. No such prevailing ethos exists today, even within America. For example, in a Gallup poll of Americans answering the question "Should America mind its own business internationally?" a full 52 percent in 2009 responded "yes," which was the highest reading since 1964. Isolationism has always been the kissing cousin of protectionism.

The maverick investor, willing to ascertain trends for what they are, not what we might wish, will regretfully conclude that macro forces present in the equity boom that commenced in the 1980s are not only missing now but are very unlikely to reappear in coming years. Slowing population, potential threats to world peace, and a mass macro movement against free markets and free trade are creating a backdrop in stark opposition to the halcyon days of the 1980s and 1990s. Because of those macro reversals, the contrarian investor must resist following the cattle stampeding off the cliff, still chasing the now-discredited cult of equities.

You *Can* Handle This Truth

Lieutenant Kaffee in *A Few Good Men* asked the right question and trapped Colonel Jessup in his own hubristic delusions. As contrarian investors, willing to buck the herd, we too must be on guard for hubris. Are equities really an appropriate investment for us? For the vast majority of investors, the honest answer to that question is "no." Bucking the Wall Street mantra of 60/40 stock/bond asset allocation and buy-and-hold takes guts, but comfort is seldom rewarded, in life or in markets. We actually *can* handle the truth, but we cannot handle the volatility. Long and strong in bonds forms a true winning, contrarian strategy.

Chapter 6

Still the One

Get Long-Term Bullish on America

In 1976, the group Orleans recorded its mega hit "Still the One." A terrific song (although the album cover features a quite creepy photo of five shirtless men from Orleans embracing), it has appeared all over the political landscape. Future U.S. Congressman John Hall wrote and performed the song. In fact, in 2004, the future Democratic Congressman Hall asked the George W. Bush campaign to stop using the catchy song in its campaign.

For much of this book, I have detailed serious U.S. problems and manias facing the global economy and investment landscape. I see a world awash in risk (and opportunity!) for those willing to take a hard, dispassionate, independent view of the world. I see international risks in China and Japan, capital risks in gold, housing, and overly owned stocks. But I also see, in the midst of these serious—even systemic—risks, incredible opportunity for America. This book, therefore, is not all a tale of woe. It is also a promise of enormous opportunity, of an America that rises phoenix-like from the ashes of global deleveraging, to maintain and expand its macro dominance in all facets: economically, politically, culturally, and militarily.

Perhaps my most contrarian, maverick position of all is a steadfast belief that America's power and dominance are young—and growing. And, like most unconventional views, this one too presents investable, actionable opportunities for the maverick thinker. Despite the torrent of negativity, both within and outside America regarding her status and future, I postulate with vigor that America remains *still the one*. In August 2011, Standard & Poor's sent shockwaves through global markets by downgrading the debt of the U.S. government from its highest AAA rating, the first such downgrade in all of American history. I pay little attention to the opinions of ratings agencies, since they lost whatever credibility they still had during the housing crisis, as they were all too willing to ignore the mammoth risks in subprime mortgages until those risks came crashing down upon the markets and the economy. Instead, their pay-to-play model allowed for winks and nods, granting Wall Street firms the "imprimatur" of the rating agencies to sell loan-shark quality paper as investment grade. Perhaps S&P views the downgrade of U.S. Treasuries as a sort of "make-up" call, but I believe their logic completely misses two crucial points. First, that America, unlike any other industrial nation, is growing demographically; we will have more workers in coming decades, not fewer like China, Germany, and Japan. Growth means an ability to shoulder debts, even one as massive as the U.S. Treasury's. Second, in times of market stress, global capital still flows straight into U.S. assets. Despite S&P protestations, capital votes with its feet, and capital comes massively into U.S. Treasuries at times of trouble.

The Right Stuff

In his epic 1979 book, *The Right Stuff*, my favorite author, Tom Wolfe, portrayed the incredible bravery and achievements of the post-WWII test pilots and early Mercury astronauts who forged America's still-extant leadership in space. My favorite story from the book surrounds Chuck Yeager breaking the sound barrier. In October 1947, Yeager became the first man to travel at the speed of sound, completing the mission in total secrecy over the California desert. Even less known, at least until Wolfe wrote about it, was that Yeager almost was medically unable to make that flight because two nights previous he broke his ribs on a drunken late-night horseback ride after a rowdy evening with fellow aviators at a hardscrabble desert bar called Pancho's Place. Talk about a truly American story! Yeager was, and is, American to the core. Because of Yeager's quintessential American-ness, Wolfe found himself fascinated. Tom Wolfe has long been an expert chronicler of trends in American society. As such, I pay particular attention to his insights, in part because I revere his acumen, and in part because many of those macro societal trends are investable, especially when they run counter to conventional wisdom.

Henry Luce famously called the twentieth century the "American century." Tom Wolfe, in a May 2008 interview, was asked if it is possible that the twenty-first century could be another American century, or is America doomed, as is largely believed, to a decline similar to that of the British Empire? He wonderfully responded:

I think we are on the edge of about 800 more years of American centuries, frankly. The biggest problem is all the people who see a problem. It's very fashionable to think that the end is near. After the end of the 20th Century, which was unquestionably the American century, American ascendancy in everything . . . was supreme in a way that no country has ever been before . . . in actual fact, there is nothing to prevent the next 8 or 9 centuries of [dominance] . . . so be happy!

When I first saw that interview, I almost leapt out of my chair. Here is an august man of letters, a respected journalist, best-selling author, and unimpeachable intellectual, sounding a rallying cry to believe in American dominance far into the future. And coming from Tom Wolfe, a Yale PhD who wears white suits and associates with the glitterati of Manhattan society, this seemingly outlandish, and incredibly contrarian, argument—that America's power is young and growing—resonates.

Before I detail my rationales and the concomitant investing opportunities, as a sort of disclaimer let me explain that my bullishness on America is not unreserved. Serious problems exist, and some grow worse, like government machinations in housing, which I detailed in Chapter 4. Nor is my bullishness the result of some jingoistic nationalism. Though I am unequivocally proud, and blessed, to call myself an American, part of what makes America so different, as I will elucidate in coming pages, is that America is not really a nation at all. At least, America is not a nation in terms of nationhood, meaning an ethnic group, a race, or a tradition-bound culture. Rather, America is an *idea*. Those who buy into America, chiefly the immigrants who continually renew and resuscitate our society, buy into the ideology of America.

Returning to Tom Wolfe, though, he is correct in noting that the fashionable crowd constantly derides America and pontificates with assurance on the alleged inevitability of America's decline as a great power. As I mentioned in Chapter 1, most Americans wrongly believe that America is either behind—or close to behind—China in sheer economic size. In fact, America's economy is four times as large. And perhaps even more remarkable, America's share of global GDP has remained amazingly constant for many decades. That is, as the world grows and expands, America keeps the pace and grows commensurately. Growth is not zero sum, of course. Dr. Mark Perry, professor at the University of Michigan and economics scholar at the American Enterprise Institute, points out that for the last 40 years, the United States has produced, in real terms, just above 25 percent of all global GDP, with considerable consistency. For example, the United States produced the same portion of global output in 2009 as it did in 1990.

Consider the massive growth of emerging markets, especially China, since 1990. And yet, does that growth come at the expense of the United States? The emphatic, and perhaps surprising, answer is "no." If anything, the growth of emerging markets has come at the expense of Europe and Japan, both of which have seen their share of global GDP erode.

I think few Americans in general, and few investment managers specifically, would have guessed that America's share of production is *not* falling. This consistency reflects the fact that America powers the global economy, both as producer and consumer, and has for decades. The idea, then, that we are witnessing a prolonged and inevitable erosion of American economic might represents folly and a foolish willingness to follow the herd. As an aside, the Middle East's share of global GDP, during those 40 years, rose from 2 percent to only 3 percent. Given the incredible flow of capital into the oil coffers those nations possess, the lack of growth is truly stunning. Moreover, that lack of growth stands as a warning against relying only on an inherent static advantage—in the case of the Middle East, crude oil. In the case of China, cheap labor. Lasting, sustained economic growth must germinate from innovation. America has shown, over decades, an uncanny ability to dynamically innovate, as I discuss in coming pages. Therein lies the secret to America's consistent dominance, a dominance that will extend far into the future, as Tom Wolfe correctly asserts.

Wolfe also said, "I really love this country. I just marvel at how good it is, and obviously it's the simple principle of freedom . . . intellectually, this is the system where people tend to experiment more and experiments are indulged . . . [but] these are terrible things to say if you want to have any standing in the intellectual world." Why is that so? Why is a confidence in America's future so unfashionable?

Perhaps one reason is that believing in the home team seems simplistic and parochial, like saying "I am from Chicago, and hence I love the Bears, end of story." But I think a more involved answer can be found historically. For whatever reason, the Western world has long held a fear and fascination when looking east toward Asia. Back in the late 1800s, Kaiser Wilhelm II of Germany coined the phrase "yellow peril" and painted a famous portrait by that name depicting St. Michael the Archangel and an allegorical Germany leading a battle against an Asiatic foe depicted as Buddha. Around the same time, in America the newspapers of William Randolph Hearst commonly used the same "yellow peril" phrase when referring to alleged Asian threats. These xenophobic, racist themes led to that time period's Chinese Exclusion Act, limiting Chinese migration to the United States. Fast forward a century later, and best-selling author Michael Crichton hit a nerve with his book, *Rising Sun,* depicting the supposedly superior tactics and Machiavellian aims of the Japanese industrial machine. For whatever inexplicable reason, Western culture has an imbedded, irrational fear of Asia. I believe that at least part of the fear of China flows from this same misguided mindset.

Another reason questioning America's global position is so fashionable is our national immaturity. George Friedman, of the forecasting firm Stratfor, uses a powerful "teenager" analogy.[1] That is, America, like a typical adolescent, has difficulty growing into its power. Like a teenager, America vacillates between illogical self-doubt and almost hubristic arrogance. I believe that once the China house of cards comes down, and America's dominance is once again as clear as it was following WWII, that we as a nation will mature into a more steadied, rational understanding of America's power. But the important point here, in terms of both global leadership and investable ideas, remains that America is a very, very *young* power, a teenager just learning to use its true faculties, with advantages that almost guarantee its primacy far into the future. I stand, therefore, as a contrarian thinker, completely afoul of the chorus on Wall Street, in the academy, and in the media, calling for—at best—a multipolar world in which America plays an important, but not leading, role. Perhaps most popular among this chorus is author Fareed Zakaria, who wrote the influential book *The Post-American World* in 2008. In fact, his book captured the cover of *Newsweek* magazine, just one stark example of the near unanimity with which the media believe in the decline of America.

While I will give *Newsweek* credit for the creativity of showing the Statue of Liberty from the rear, indicating promise *elsewhere* in the world rather than in America, I would also suggest that few Americans immigrate elsewhere, while millions, legal and illegal, still swarm the borders of America. The masses vote, therefore, as they have for centuries—with their feet. And those votes have gone, and will continue to flow, to America first and foremost, to the world's dominant and growing superpower, the nation with "The Right Stuff."

American Glasnost

In the late 1980s, as America turned up the military and economic pressure on the wizened Soviet Empire, Premier Mikhail Gorbachev attempted a partial relaxation of communist rule, a process he called glasnost. In Russian the word means a spirit of openness and transparency. Accordingly, in the USSR censorship relaxed, political prisoners were released, and limited free enterprise took hold. This partial openness, of course, failed to truly transform Soviet society and merely delayed the inevitable breakup of the Soviet system. In many ways, Russia today is regressing away from glasnost toward an ever more repressive model of crony capitalism predicated upon energy production and little else. But the real version of glasnost, real openness and transparency, is found to a greater extent in America than anywhere else on earth. And this transparency represents a systemic reason why America has succeeded so mightily in the past and will persist in dominating the future.

I admit, transparency is not a uniquely American attribute. Clearly, European systems, too, treasure openness and allow for nearly unmitigated flow of communication and freedom of thought. But America does stand alone in its willingness to experiment, to self-examine, and to admit failure and make recompense. In terms of experimentation, America dominates the processes that lead to breakthrough successes in business, the sciences, and finance. If you think of truly game-changing products and companies, nearly the entire list of such advances emanates from America.

Take, for example, Google. Its co-founder Sergey Brin came to America as a six-year-old child from his native Russia. Though his father succeeded in school as a brilliant mathematician, the anti-Jewish strictures of the Soviet system precluded his advancement on to graduate programs. The Brins lived a meager and unhappy existence in Moscow before deciding to emigrate and reach America. In the year 2000, Sergey would say of his parents: "I know the hard times that my parents went through there, and am very thankful that I was brought to the States."[2] Following in his father's footsteps, he excelled in mathematics. Unlike his father, his brilliance was rewarded with admission to Stanford University's prestigious graduate program in computer science. While there, he met fellow Ph.D. student Larry Page, and they began developing their own data mining services using computers in their dorm rooms. They soon realized the superiority of their new search engines and left Stanford with financial backing from professors and Silicon Valley executives. The company they founded, Google, has a market capitalization well above $100 billion, and Sergey's personal wealth is estimated by Forbes in 2011 as nearly $20 billion. About the company he co-created, the *Economist* magazine raved:

In 1440, Johannes Gutenberg introduced Europe to the mechanical printing press, printing Bibles for mass consumption. The technology allowed for books and manuscripts—originally replicated by hand—to be printed at a much faster rate, thus spreading knowledge and helping to usher in the European Renaissance . . . Google has done a similar job.[3]

Brin's life represents a classic "only in America" story. And why only in America? Because America alone combines all the facets needed to produce a truly revolutionary process that changes lifestyles, customs, and creates serious wealth. In this case, first and foremost the willingness to accept immigrants. Secondly, the meritocratic nature of American higher education. And third, the openness—the glasnost—allowing for a couple of poor graduate students to tinker and experiment with bold new ideas.

The Microsoft story in some ways parallels the Google one, albeit a generation earlier. Like Brin, Bill Gates was a brilliant young man, obsessed with tinkering with computers while a student. As an undergraduate at Harvard University, Bill Gates spent countless hours programming until he and his friend, Paul Allen, grew convinced they could start a powerful software firm. His company soon flourished and became the dominant operating system globally for the exploding personal computer market. At its height, Microsoft grew into the world's largest company with Bill Gates as the world's richest man.

Take a look at the photo of the Microsoft team in 1978 (Figure 6.1). Bill Gates is in the lower left of the picture, the one who looks like he is 12 years old, instead of 23 at the time. Only in a country as meritocratic as America would someone who looks like a 12-year-old be able to found a corporate Goliath.

Though his story might appear less dramatic than Brin's, his tale also represents an "only in America" reality. For example, though his family was moderately well-off, he boasted no particular connections, no status or political relevance. And he left one of the most prestigious universities in the world to pursue his business dream. In China, for example, a budding Bill Gates had better make sure he greases the right palms in the communist party, because such unbridled entrepreneurship would simply not be tolerated. Further, the idea of leaving a highly coveted university spot, to take on the kind of reputational risk of leaving a Harvard-status school and possibly failing, would likely prove impossible to a culture obsessed with saving face and avoiding failures.

In sharp contrast, America's transparency allows for failure, and in fact almost seems to encourage it! As long as that failure results in further attempts at self-improvement, American culture actually revels in the

Figure 6.1   Microsoft, in 1978
SOURCE: Microsoft.

comeback story. The United States is the country of second and third—
and tenth—chances. That characteristic represents a uniquely American
attribute. Donald Trump, with all his brashness and bravado, also presents a uniquely American story. During the 1970s and 1980s Trump
saw opportunity in New York City, well before it became obvious that
Manhattan would revive from the moribund days of the city's financial
crisis and become far more livable and prosperous. He invested heavily,
mostly through substantial borrowing, in myriad New York real estate
projects. His first big success was transforming the dilapidated
Commodore Hotel near Grand Central Station into the Grand Hyatt
hotel. That heavy borrowing came crashing down on Trump in the
early 1990s recession, when he was forced to declare business bankruptcy and nearly personal bankruptcy. At his financial low point,
Trump personally owed hundreds of millions of dollars. But by the late

1990s, undeterred by his years of problems, he emerged once again not only as a cultural force, a true commercial brand, but also as a major real estate mogul. In 2011, Forbes estimated his net worth at \$2.7 billion. Trump's tale of success, failure, and regeneration, conveys a uniquely American quality.

Speaking of failure and regeneration, Thomas Watson's life is also worth a brief mention. Born to a modest farm family in New York State, Watson worked an array of unsuccessful sales jobs as a young man, peddling everything from pianos to sewing machines. He eventually became a butcher. The butcher shop failed, leaving him jobless and penniless at age 22. When he returned his butcher shop NCR cash register back to the company, he grew intrigued with the company and hounded NCR for a job. After a superbly successful career as an NCR salesman, at 40 years old he joined the small but fast growing forerunner to IBM. He eventually took charge and spearheaded phenomenal growth. By 1952, IBM controlled fully 90 percent of the tabulating machines in America. When he died in 1956, IBM had over 70,000 employees. His motto, which persists to this day within IBM—*THINK*—is terrific advice for anyone with a contrarian bent. And, once again, Watson represents the best of America's openness and willingness to tolerate tinkering, failure, and the admired comeback story, in this case from failed butcher to technology titan.

That American glasnost provides the spark necessary for a culture of innovation unparalleled anywhere else in the world. In fact, Thomas Watson's IBM remains a steadfast global leader in the business of innovations. For many years, it has registered more patents than any organization in the world, in 2009 filing an incredible 4,169 of them. Other American firms like Intel, Microsoft, and Hewlett-Packard can also be found in the top 10, but not one Chinese firm. America is the country that split the atom, and decades later invented Facebook. The culture of innovation resonates and dominates in America. Far from a cut-and-paste model like China, or the central industrial planning system of Japan, American glasnost means true openness, tolerance of failure, and unencumbered tinkering. For that reason, American research and development remains the envy of the globe, and the systemic and cultural advantages of America ensure that dominance far into the future. Though blessed with abundant natural resources, the United States has never relied on a static inherent advantage, like the Kuwaitis with oil or the Chinese with cheap labor or Jamaica with beautiful beaches. Instead, innovation forms the backbone of American enterprise.

Much, even most, of that innovation results from new Americans, from the continual, regenerating flow of people and ideas from the entire globe to American shores. Fully 50 percent of all patents registered in the United States came from foreign-born people. This preponderance is not surprising, given that an amazing 80 percent of all U.S. graduate students in math are foreigners. Critics of America often deride that heavy international concentration of math and science graduate students. In reality, we should laud and celebrate the trend of the world's best minds coming to America for advanced study. In 2004, the children of immigrants made up 65 percent of the Math Olympiad's top scorers, and 46 percent of the U.S. Physics Team. That same year, children of immigrants represented 60 percent of the finalists and seven of the top ten final winners of the prestigious national Intel Science Talent Search.[4] I view these trends as yet another proof of the incredible attraction of the American way. For the best minds, the best ideas, and the most motivated people in the world, there is only one destination in the end, and it is America. In coming pages I will explain more about how immigration forms the most enduring and unique of all America's attributes, but for now suffice it to acknowledge that American innovation thrives because it is truly the whole world's innovation, brought to fruition in the global laboratory we call the United States. This country possesses the culture, the schools, the tolerance, the capital, and the transparency to allow innovation to flourish.

As further proof of the dominance of American innovation, consider the field of Nobel Prizes. In my opening chapter, I mentioned the basketball Dream Team from the 1992 Barcelona Olympics. As dominant as that team was on the hard court, almost as dominant (and a lot more important) is America's success over in Sweden collecting endless Nobel Prizes, 326 in total so far. The United States has won almost three times as many Nobel Prizes as the next closest country, and the pace of awards continues unabated, from literature to economics to physics. As impressive, 10 of the most recent 25 American Nobel winners were foreign-born. Once again, the world's talent comes here. Using basketball as a reference, the best players in the world, whether from Germany or Argentina, choose to compete in the world's best market and the National Basketball Association, and so too do the world's top thinkers choose to "play" in the United States. By comparison, China has received only two Nobel Prizes ever, both for peace. The first winner, the Dalai Lama, is not allowed to speak or travel freely in China. The second, Liu Xiaobo, sits as I write in a Chinese jail, a prisoner of conscience. I will bet on the United States with its long, storied list of top scientists and thinkers rather than betting on the Chinese regime that censors and abuses freedom of thought. Such a system has never, and won't ever, produce real innovation.

Human Growth

In recent years, professional sports, especially baseball, have endured serious scandals regarding Human Growth Hormone (HGH) as stars from Barry Bonds to Mark McGwire have come under much scrutiny regarding their use of performance enhancing substances. The goal of HGH, of course, is growth—getting bigger, faster, stronger. Well, America as a country is, thankfully, taking its own form of HGH. Because of the attributes unique to America—such as transparency and innovation—America is growing in every way, economically and demographically. It is hard to exaggerate how important this fact is.

America is truly alone in the world as the only major industrial power that is growing, both economically and in people. As I stated earlier in the book, there exist no shortcuts to growth—no "fairy dust." An economy grows from either more people or more productivity, and preferably both as in America's case. China is growing but its population is about to crest. Japan is barely growing and its population is racing toward implosion; the same for Italy and Spain. Even Germany, considered to be our chief European economic peer, faces a future as a far smaller country, in every way. Today, Germany has just over 80 million people, but by 2060 it will decline by 20 percent to just above 60 million, a truly staggering decline.[5] You might be saying, "But Germans are so productive, can't they still furnish great output from a smaller populace?" In fact, German productive superiority is a myth. Not that Germany is unproductive—they are well above the global trend in productivity. But Germany stands well below the United States in GDP produced per hour of work, and even below France, a country far more renowned for beauty and culture than productivity.[6] Combine a smaller population with inferior productivity, and the mega trends make clear the projection that America, not Germany, and surely not China, will dominate the twenty-first century. Demographics, after all, are indeed destiny. Demographics simply cannot change rapidly once trends assert themselves. Once population starts to recede, the math simply works against growth, and for a society to reverse the decline is akin to a person turning around a supertanker in the ocean using a canoe paddle. Going forward, what will demand for housing be like in a shrinking Germany? For that matter, where will China find new cheap labor, now that it has reached the Lewis Point of exhausting easily exploitable rural workers? And how will a Japanese consumer firm market children's products to a nation unwilling to reproduce?

Thankfully, the situation in America represents the opposite future, one of growth. America boasts a far higher native-born rate of reproduction plus boundless immigration, legal and illegal, solidifying a future trend of growth—a country that can, and should, become a superpower of a half-billion people.

Growth in people represents not only more demand and a larger market, but also the key advantages of scale. I think we pay too little attention to the advantages of the massive size of America. For example, Wal-Mart grew into one of the largest companies and employers in the world before it made any serious venture overseas. It did, of course, eventually extend its business globally, but the point is that it first prospered on a giant scale only within the United States, because of the mammoth size of the American market. In contrast, a growing company in, say, Norway, no matter how innovative, simply must seek other markets to truly scale up profits. In fact, that fictional Norwegian company must, and will, inevitably, direct its efforts to selling into— where else?—America, the world's largest market.

Scale also allows for flexibility unknown to most economies. Ireland provides a dour example of the problems of lack of scale. Until 2007, Ireland was widely regarded as the boom country of Europe, often called the "Celtic tiger." Sadly, after the credit crisis, Ireland and its banks are in a tailspin going lower, resembling more a Gaelic kitten than a Celtic tiger. The whole island grew quickly on the backs of property speculation and building, not unlike Las Vegas, Nevada, in the United States. But in Las Vegas, the laid-off roofer can easily move to another part of the country that is prospering, such as Texas or North Dakota. Those regions in 2011 have benefitted from an energy boom, enjoy near full employment, and are building homes at a still rapid rate. America is a huge country, rarely growing or receding all at once. In the early 1990s the defense budget fell and California suffered badly, far worse than the rest of the country in the 1991–1992 recession, seeing its property markets fall as much as 30 percent and joblessness rise. What unfolded was a mass exodus of people to neighboring states, especially in the Northwest and Arizona. Those faster-growing areas attracted the talent and aspirations from California, and so America's scale greatly reduced the net economic pain of that recession. For the jobless construction worker in Ireland today in 2011, no such option exists. With only about 4.5 million people in the Republic of Ireland, it simply lacks scale. In addition, although the alleged unity of the European Union is promoted heavily by Brussels bureaucrats and the media, the reality indicates that an Irish construction worker may have a very difficult time finding work in a more prospering France, for example, as language and cultural barriers make that move nettlesome.

Similarly, out-of-work Spaniards, where the unemployment rate is an alarming 20 percent, are not flocking en masse to the growing Germany, as it is simply too difficult a transition. So while the EU compares favorably to the United States in population and GDP, it in reality represents a far smaller scale market than America. In the United States, unemployed workers in Michigan have little transition trouble moving to Texas for work. Moreover, looking again at Ireland, due to its small size and concomitant lack of economic diversity, the whole of the island suffers at once from the same financial ailment: overcapacity and leverage in real estate.

Size matters, and scale provides both mass opportunity for new products during good times and protection against concentration of risks in bad times. No need for HGH for America, since the country is growing strongly, especially demographically, and therefore presents the world's most important, dynamic market.

They're Coming to America

Throughout this chapter, I have alluded to the impact of immigration. I believe we really cannot overemphasize the unique benefit massive immigration provides America now, and will well into the future. Neil Diamond might be best known for his cheesy sequin bedazzled shirts on stage. But he has also sold well over 100 million albums and clearly captured the imagination of legions. The son of immigrants, he certainly captured the spirit of the United States in his anthem "America," singing about a waving flag welcoming the world's teeming masses to our shores. Indeed they do arrive, every single day on the water and in the air, both poor migrant workers seeking jobs in sweltering produce fields and brilliant PhD students en route to the laboratories of Stanford University. Both legal and illegal, the world's masses vote with their feet continually and they still select America as the destination of choice, the only place in the world offering real opportunity to immigrants.

America, after all, is truly defined by immigration, by its willingness and tolerance to accept newcomers, and the guts and determination of those risk-taking migrants willing to leap into the American ideal. No country in the world even resembles America in this regard. For all its vaunted growth, China sees no queue forming to enter from abroad. Japan's aversion to foreigners precludes any such migration. And the immigration Europe does tolerate represents far more a political and cultural hurdle than an attribute, since the mostly Muslim newcomers live very separate lives from the native-born French, Dutch, and Germans. Sergey Brin of Google, an immigrant, became one of the richest people in America before the age of 40. Tom Wolfe commented on this tolerance of immigrants in a *Wall Street Journal* interview, saying America is:

. . . really the only democratic country in the world. Find me one country, just one country in the entire world that would let a foreign people, different culture, different language, and in many cases different color than the majority of the native stock take over politically an entire metropolitan area in less than one generation. I'm talking about the Cubans in Miami.[7]

Indeed, traveling to Miami today, one feels as much in Latin America as in the United States on the surface. But scratch beneath the veneer of a different language and some actually insignificant cultural dissimilarities, and Miami is actually a fully American place, committed to the ideals that make America unique: capitalism, tolerance, transparency, innovation, democracy—and in ways that no Latin American city could even resemble. This openness to newcomers, new ideas, and global capital forges a dynamism that makes America truly unique among the world's economies. Ronald Reagan spoke eloquently on this American attribute when he remarked in his 1989 Farewell Address that America was:

*. . . a tall, proud city built on rocks stronger than oceans,
wind-swept, God-blessed, and teeming with people of all
kinds living in harmony and peace; a city with free ports that
hummed with commerce and creativity. And if there had to
be city walls, the walls had doors and the doors were open to
anyone with the will and the heart to get here.*

A master of imagery, President Reagan understood the importance
of America's openness. Note in that paragraph he speaks of ports and
trade and immigration—ideas and practices unique to the American
experience.

This status as the primary destination for the world's best and brightest will only become more material in the years ahead. This book lays
out the case for global economic turmoil and deleveraging. If I am even
partially right about the troubles facing China and other emerging
markets, about the overcapacity in the world and the painful deflationary pressures ahead, then the world's talent—and capital—will en masse
seek a better home. I submit that no other place will compete for that
talent and capital better than the United States. Global economic turmoil
will necessitate a massive flight toward the United States. I imagine the
young aggressive engineer in China, who has tasted an imperfect form
of capitalism, yearning for the actual real thing once the Chinese mirage
starts to unfurl. Similarly, a talented high-rise construction manager in
Dubai will, once deflation ravages his commodity-dependent homeland,
seek opportunity in the only place offering true freedom and lasting
economic opportunity: America. While America is sure to suffer greatly
from a mass emerging market capital drawdown, eventually America
will rise off the mat the only lasting winner out of the chaos, the one
giant able to withstand the blows and then emerge stronger than ever,
particularly relative to the rest of the world.

America's promise does not, of course, present an opportunity
without risks. For example, although America has always been a nation

of immigrants, it has also paradoxically long harbored significant anti-immigrant sentiments. From the anti-Catholic "Know Nothing" political party of the mid-1800s to the present-day harsh anti-immigrant state statutes in Arizona, opposition to immigration represents a significant voice in American culture and politics. And politically speaking, this aversion to the new is found in equal parts on the Left and the Right. Democrat-leaning unions oppose immigration as mightily as isolationist traditionalists like Pat Buchanan within the Republican Party. Further, during poor economic times the natural inclination is to circle the wagons and become *less* open in every way: trade, immigration, and so on. The natural instinct is to "protect what we got." But in fact, the superior, thoughtful reaction in times of turmoil is to grow ever more open, because the world's talent and capital will, having been burned in China and elsewhere, seek the safety and opportunity that only America affords. To be sure, serious resistance exists within America to such openness to new talent, as evidenced by the recent retracements in the availability of H1B visas for highly skilled immigrants. So I do not expect this influx of talent to flow seamlessly. But, using history as a guide, the more open and dynamic forces of American society will prevail and, through difficulties, ultimately welcome the world's minds and capital.

Regarding safety, I believe we have paid too little attention in recent decades to America's military superiority. Because this golden age for equities has been marked by relative global peace, we forget too easily that the preponderance of human history is marked not by peace but by conflict. We would be foolish to believe that humanity has somehow evolved into a permanent post-conflict era. Indeed, violent conflagrations often arise out of economic turmoil. For example, World War II followed on the heels of the Great Depression. I believe this present economic dislocation from the credit crisis is sure to result in actual armed conflict on a scale unseen in decades. Precisely where and when these struggles will arise remains very hard to predict, but I am confident in predicting that they *will* commence. And if/when they do commence, global capital will swiftly flee to the relative safety of America. The United States spends almost as much on its military as the rest of the world combined. Across the entire globe, no ship sails, or plane flies, without the implicit permission of the U.S. military. Partly because of this military dominance, I believe the U.S. dollar will remain the world's reserve currency far into the future. Despite all the carping in the media and among elites about the dollar's assured diminution, it is still used today in 85 percent of the world's transactions. Clearly, part of the dollar primacy is the inherent backing of the U.S. military, something that no other country in the world can even come close to securing, and won't for decades into the future. In 2011, the global media made much of the fact that China is finally launching its first aircraft carrier. Allegedly, this ship marks the first salvo in China's arrival as a military power, the first time it can project power beyond its immediate sphere. In point of fact, though, aircraft carriers are now approximately 80-year-old technology! Our very elderly grandfathers flew on them. Sorry, China, but I am not about to start shaking because you have a total of one carrier. The United States has 11, and has since poodle skirts were fashionable. Moreover, and perhaps even more importantly, simply floating a giant ship does not secure power. The technology and training and manpower required to actually use the potential of a carrier takes generations, not months. I seriously doubt that China will be able to effectively use its new carrier for real power projection for many years. In contrast, the functionality and incredible lethality of the American carriers is unquestioned. And that military dominance guarantees, far into the future, that capital seeking safety will always defer to America.

Love Your Mother (Meaning the U.S. Dollar)

The U.S. dollar reminds me of a parent, often underappreciated by children except in times of real need. Despite the almost incessantly anti-dollar carping of the financial media and Wall Street, the U.S. dollar truly represents the "mother's milk" of all investments, a basis for stable growth. Right now the U.S. dollar presents, I think, the best opportunity for the contrarian investor to capitalize on all the themes of this chapter and, indeed, this whole book. In a world awash in risk, beset by deflationary pressures, and far too pessimistic on America's prospects, the U.S. dollar represents a woefully under-owned and underappreciated asset. I see years and decades of dollar strength ahead as the emerging market dream becomes closer to a nightmare, Japan's inevitable implosion accelerates, and gold loses its luster as an alternative. In fact, I predict that the dollar will, in coming years, again trade to parity versus both the euro and the British pound. Figure 6.2 shows a two-decade graph of the euro currency versus the U.S. dollar.

In October 2001, the euro hit a low of .8228 euros per U.S. dollar, before beginning a protracted march higher to well above 1.50 euros per U.S. dollar. Though the euro has not traded at 1-to-1 parity versus the U.S. dollar since December 2002, we believe that markets will see that price again soon.

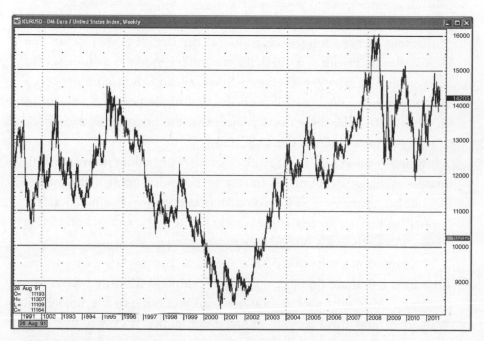

Figure 6.2   Euro Currency per U.S. Dollar Back 20 Years

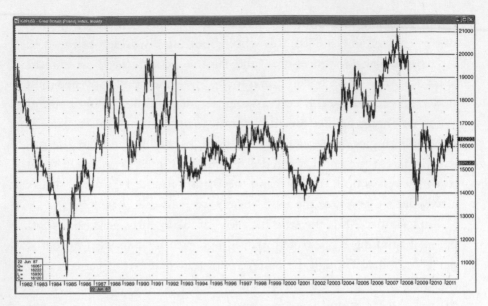

Figure 6.3   British Pound per U.S. Dollar Back 30 Years

Taking an even longer term look at the British pound versus the U.S. dollar in Figure 6.3, back in the mid-1980s the pound traded nearly down to parity with the U.S. dollar, and then commenced a quarter-century rally, reaching above 2 pounds per U.S. dollar in October 2007. Like the euro, I project that the pound will trade back to parity at 1-to-1 versus the U.S. dollar.

Whether using ETFs that track currencies or trading futures or cash foreign exchange accounts, a consistent policy of going long on the U.S. dollar provides a key trading opportunity for the independent thinker willing to ascertain the world's true risks and acknowledge America's systemic advantages.

I admit that I reflexively love America. But my views regarding America's economic primacy flow not from nationalism but from dispassionate analysis of present conventional wisdom—in the media, on Wall Street, and in academia—and recognizing the flaws of logic inherent in that "America in decline" thinking. I would not invest, nor recommend investing, based on a visceral admiration for America.

Rather, the world's present economic circumstances provide a chance to profit from something I dearly love, the United States of America. I remain convinced that this stance, this belief that America's power is young and growing, represents my most important and most contrarian view of all. As I think about America and its investing potential, I start to hum that Orleans song from way back when—America is still having fun, and we're still the one.

Conclusion

In the introduction to this book I mentioned the derivation of the term "maverick," which came from a Texas land baron in the 1800s. Another Old West mention might illuminate my skepticism regarding the masses. The northern plains Indians, in the days when plentiful bison roamed the West, used a brutal but effective hunting technique called a "buffalo jump." This practice was first described by Meriwether Lewis of the famed Lewis and Clark Expedition. The Indians would drive the buffalo into a stampede and trick them into stampeding off a cliff, killing themselves in the fall. Talk about danger in following the herd! I submit that the financial version of the buffalo jump was inflicted upon many investors in the recent credit crunch. And not long before that, many endured similar pain in the dot-com bubble at the turn of the millennium. The point is, be wary of the crowd. Think independently. Be willing to discern and to act differently, often in outright defiance of supposed mass wisdom. Be aware that in this digital age of near constant connectivity, the proclivity

175

toward dangerous group-think grows apace, and so too must our skepticism and independence strengthen.

I see a world abounding in risks, particularly in Asia, where both China and Japan present massive macro threats to the global economy. In America I see too many people still too much invested in equities and hiding in the dangerous, speculative gold theme. I foresee a world very different from the last quarter-century, in which demographics and a preponderance of world peace almost guaranteed benevolent financial markets. Therefore be watchful and properly skeptical, be aware that *SS Eastland*-like dangers may exist in a financial form, and that following the herd uncritically may result in very unpleasant outcomes.

But a world abounding in risks also means a world abounding in opportunity. More than anything else, consider my grand thesis: that out of the global ashes, only America will truly persevere and thrive. America's singular and unique attributes—demographic growth, innovative culture, contract law, geographic advantages, military superiority—all virtually guarantee America's status as the world's sole economic, cultural, military, and political superpower for the rest of the century. Be prepared, therefore, to go very long on America once the inevitable emerging market collapse unfolds.

Notes

Introduction

1. Jack Woodford, *The Autobiography of Jack Woodford* (Seattle, WA: Woodford Memorial Editions, 1962).

Chapter 1   The Corleones Meet Confucius

1. George Friedman, *The Next 100 Years: A Forecast for the 21st Century* (New York: Doubleday, 2009), location 1512.
2. Kathy Chu, "Most Americans Think China No. 1 Economy: It Isn't," *USA Today*, February 14, 2011.
3. *The Wealth of Nations*, Book IV, Chapter II, 456. Adam Smith, Digireads and Lawrence, KS.
4. CNBC, December 10, 2010. CNBC Squawk Box.
5. Michael Wines, "China Fortifies State Business to Fuel Growth," *New York Times*, August 29, 2010.
6. Ibid.
7. Yu Yongding, "A Different Road Forward," *China Daily*, December 23, 2010, www.chinadaily.com.cn/opinion/2010-12/23/content_11742757.htm.

8. A. Gary Shilling, *The Age of Deleveraging: Investment Strategies for a Decade of Slow Growth and Deflation* (Hoboken, NJ: John Wiley & Sons, 2011), location 6908.

9. Pivot Capital Management Report, "China's Investment Boom," 2009.

10. "Ordos, China: A Modern Ghost Town," slide show on Time.com, www.time.com/time/photogallery/0,29307,1975397,00.html#ixzz1FPJYlgp7.

11. David M. Smick, *The World Is Curved: Hidden Dangers to the Global Economy* (New York: Portfolio, 2008), location 4531.

12. David Barboza, "China, New Land of Shoppers, Builds Malls on Gigantic Scale," *New York Times*, May 25, 2005.

13. Shilling, *Age of Deleveraging*, location 7252.

14. Louis Bedigian, "Jim Chanos: Big Misconception That Chinese Government Can Do What It Wants," February 10, 2011, www.benzinga.com/media/cnbc/11/02/849958/jim-chanos-big-misconception-that-chinese-government-can-do-what-it-wants.

15. David Barboza, "Contrarian Investor Sees Economic Crash in China," *New York Times*, January 7, 2010, www.nytimes.com/2010/01/08/business/global/08chanos.html.

16. Bill Powell, "Chanos vs. China," *Fortune*, November 17, 2010, http://finance.fortune.cnn.com/2010/11/17/chanos-vs-china/.

17. Hugo Restall, "China's Real Estate Frenzy," *Wall Street Journal*, December 26, 2010.

18. Pivot Capital Management Report, "China's Investment Boom," 2009.

19. "Chanos vs. China (Part Two)," January 13, 2011, http://fortune-china.blogspot.com/2011/01/chanos-vs-china-part-two-fortune-china.html.

20. U.S. Census Bureau, International Database.

21. Credit Suisse, "China: The Turning Point of the Labour Market," January 5, 2011.

22. Calum MacLeod, "China May Relax Its One-Child Rule," *USA Today*, September 10, 2010, www.usatoday.com/news/world/2010-09-09-1Achinaonechild09_ST_N.htm.

23. Geoff Dyer, "End Looms for Era of Cheap Chinese Labour," *Financial Times*, June 3, 2010, www.ft.com/cms/s/0/ecca5704-6f01-11df-a2f7-00144feabdc0.html.

24. Scott Malone, "Surging China Costs Turn Some U.S. Makers Homeward," July 1, 2011, www.foxbusiness.com/industries/2011/06/28/surging-china-costs-turn-some-us-makers-homeward/.

25. Bill Powell, "The End of Cheap Labor in China," *Time*, June 26, 2011, www.time.com/time/magazine/article/0,9171,2078121,00.html.

26. Credit Suisse, "China: Turning Point."

27. Bloomberg News, "Consumer Spending Fades in China Economy after 'Peak Days,'" June 17, 2011, www.bloomberg.com/news/2011-06-16/consumers -fade-in-china-economy-racked-by-inflation-with-peak-days-gone.html.

28. "China Faces Growing Gender Imbalance," BBC News, January 11, 2010, http://news.bbc.co.uk/2/hi/asia-pacific/8451289.stm.

29. Bloomberg News, "Facebook Users Dodge Censors to Climb Over China Great Firewall," February 17, 2011, http://noir.bloomberg.com/apps/news ?pid=newsarchive&sid=aKcpYrjbxXdA.

30. James Surowiecki, "Don't Enter the Dragon," January 31, 2011, www .newyorker.com/talk/financial/2011/01/31/110131ta_talk_surowiecki.

31. Tim Worstall, "Sino Forest: Is This the Biggest Theft in History?" June 20, 2011, http://blogs.forbes.com/timworstall/2011/06/20/sino-forest-is-this-the -biggest-theft-in-history/.

32. Andrew Jacobs, "China's Army of Graduates Struggles for Jobs," December 11, 2010, www.nytimes.com/2010/12/12/world/asia/12beijing.html ?pagewanted=1.

33. Pivot Capital Management Report, "China's Investment Boom," 2009.

34. http://extremecapitalists.com/.

35. "Hong Kong Phew-Whee: Our Quarterly Index Reveals the World's Most Overvalued Homes," *Economist*, March 3, 2011, www.economist.com/node/ 18285595?story_id=18285595&CFID=159690140&CFTOKEN=65413962.

Chapter 2 Dolls Are Meant for Children

1. Duncan Bartlett, "Japan's Toys for the Elderly," BBC News, April 30, 2006, http://news.bbc.co.uk/2/hi/business/4919606.stm.

2. Lee Brodie, "Dennis Gartman: Forget EU, Bigger Debt Crisis Brewing Elsewhere," May 18, 2011, www.cnbc.com/id/43082980.

3. Gregg Easterbrook, "China as Number One? Remember Japan in the '80s," Reuters, August 18, 2010, http://blogs.reuters.com/gregg-easterbrook/2010/ 08/18/china-as-number-one-remember-japan-in-the-80s/.

4. Lester Thurow, *Head to Head: The Coming Economic Battle among Japan, Europe and America* (New York: William Morrow, 1992).

5. A. Gary Shilling, *The Age of Deleveraging* (Hoboken, NJ: John Wiley & Sons, 2010), location 1171.

6. John Mauldin and Jonathan Tepper, *Endgame: The End of the Debt SuperCycle and How It Changes Everything* (Hoboken, NJ: John Wiley & Sons, 2011), location 4180.

7. George Friedman, *The Next 100 Years: A Forecast for the 21st Century* (New York: Doubleday, 2009), 93.

8. Mauldin and Tepper, *Endgame*, location 4163.

9. Ibid., location 3490.

10. Ibid., location 4180.

11. Kyle Bass (Heyman Capital), "Waiting for 'X-Day' for Japan," February 19, 2011, www.gurufocus.com/news.php?id=123040.

12. Rie Ishiguro and Leika Kihara, "FACTBOX-Policymakers' Key Quotes on Japan Fiscal Policy," Reuters, June 21, 2010, www.reuters.com/article/2010/06/21/japan-economy-quotes-idUSTOE65K04I20100621.

13. Julian Ryall, "Third of Young Japanese Men Not Interested in Sex," January 13, 2011, *Telegraph*, www.telegraph.co.uk/news/worldnews/asia/japan/8257400/Third-of-young-Japanese-men-not-interested-in-sex.html.

14. Paul Sheard, "For Japan, This Could Be Turning Point for the Better," *Bangkok Post*, April 11, 2011, www.bangkokpost.com/business/economics/231386/for-japan-this-could-be-turning-point-for-the-better.

15. Kevin Crowley, "Eclectica's Hendry Turns Greece Profit into China Failure Wager," Bloomberg, January 9, 2011, www.bloomberg.com/news/2011-01-10/eclectica-s-hendry-turns-greece-chaos-profit-into-bet-that-china-will-fail.html.

Chapter 3   Can't Touch This

1. Romans 6:23.

2. Steve Liesman, "Why the Fed Is So Reluctant to Head Off Inflation Threat," April 15, 2011, www.cnbc.com/id/42595125/Why_the_Fed_Is_So_Reluctant_to_Head_Off_Inflation_Threat.

3. John Melloy, "Double Take: Inflation for Majority of Economy at Record Lows," April 20, 2011, www.cnbc.com/id/42663205/.

4. Remarks by Governor Ben S. Bernanke Before the National Economists Club, Washington, D.C., November 21, 2002. Deflation: Making Sure "It" Doesn't Happen Here.

5. Willem Buiter, "Gold—A Six-Thousand-Year-Old Bubble," November 8, 2009, http://blogs.ft.com/maverecon/2009/11/gold-a-six-thousand-year-old-bubble/#axzz1Sm5NZVdE.

6. Carolyn Cui, Liam Pleven, and Ray Brindal, "As Gold Climbs, So Do the Deals," September 3, 2010, http://online.wsj.com/article/SB10001424052748704855104575469982112990238.html.

7. Adam Katz, "Gold as an Investment? Think Again," May 2, 2008, http://seekingalpha.com/article/75325-gold-as-an-investment-think-again.

8. Nicholas Larkin, "Gold Rallying to $1,500 as Soros's Bubble Inflates," August 31, 2010, www.bloomberg.com/news/2010-08-30/gold-rallying-to-1-500 -for-analysts-as-soros-s-bubble-inflates.html.

Chapter 4 House of Pain

1. John Carney, "Here's How the Community Reinvestment Act Led to the Housing Bubble's Lax Lending," *Business Insider,* June 27, 2009, www .businessinsider.com/the-cra-debate-a-users-guide-2009-6.
2. Ben Bernanke, "The Community Reinvestment Act: Its Evolution and New Challenges," speech, March 30, 2007, www.federalreserve.gov/newsevents/ speech/bernanke20070330a.htm.
3. Press briefing, December 8, 1993, http://clinton6.nara.gov/1993/12/1993 -12-08-briefing-by-bentsen-and-rubin.text.html.
4. Bernanke, "Community Reinvestment Act."
5. Daniel Indiviglio, "5 Ways the Government Screws Up Housing Finance," March 27, 2011, www.theatlantic.com/business/archive/2011/03/5-ways-the -government-screws-up-housing-finance/73068/.
6. Mortimer Zuckerman, "The American Dream of Home Ownership Has Become a Nightmare," *U.S. News & World Report*, September 23, 2010.
7. John Mauldin, "Don't Look for Housing to Help the Economy, Says Schilling," May 17, 2011, www.forbes.com.
8. Diana Olick, "No Housing Recovery without Private Label Mortgage Investors," May 18, 2011, www.cnbc.com.
9. Tamara Keith, "What's Next: Life after Fannie and Freddie," April 30, 2011, www.npr.org.
10. Shahien Nasiripour, "75% of Homeowners in Obama's Loan Modification Plan Still Owe More Than Their Homes Are Worth," April 14, 2011, www .huffingtonpost.com.
11. Michael Lewis, "Betting on the Blind Side," *Vanity Fair*, April 2011.
12. Marc Hogan, "Is Housing Out of the Woods?" *Bloomberg Businessweek*, October 23, 2006.
13. Michael Lewis, *The Big Short: Inside the Doomsday Machine* (New York: W.W. Norton, 2010), 55.
14. Brett Arends, "How to Bet Like John Paulson," *Wall Street Journal*, October 1, 2010.
15. Zuckerman, "American Dream of Home Ownership."
16. Ibid.
17. Rob Reuteman, "Vacation-Home Market Faces Long Road to Recovery," *USA Today,* May 8, 2011, www.usatoday.com/money/economy/housing/2011 -05-08-cnbc-vacation-homes_n.htm.

18. Kathleen Howley, "Americans Shun Most Affordable Homes in Generation as Owning Loses Appeal," April 19, 2011, www.bloomberg.com.

19. Zuckerman, "American Dream of Home Ownership."

20. John Carney, "Housing Crash 2.0 Is Accelerating," April 26, 2011, www.cnbc.com.

21. Jeff Manning, "Another Symptom of the Downturn: Unpaid Fees at Housing Associations," *Oregonian,* April 18, 2011.

22. Paul Starobin, "A Dream Endangered. (Yeah, So?)" March 24, 2011, www.nationaljournal.com.

23. Nick Timiraos and Dawn Wotapka, "Home Market Takes a Tumble," *Wall Street Journal,* May 9, 2011.

24. David Lynch, "Phoenix's Underwater Mortgages Show Weakness in Housing Threatens Recovery," April 27, 2011, www.bloomberg.com.

25. Anthony Mirhaydari, "Why Home Prices Are Falling—Again," May 18, 2011, www.msn.com.

26. Martin Andelman, "NBC/MSNBC.com Try to Cover the Foreclosure Crisis," June 10, 2011, www.mandelman.ml-implode.com.

27. Reuteman, "Vacation-Home Market."

28. Zuckerman, "American Dream of Home Ownership."

29. Steve Matthews, "New Households Form at Fastest Rate since '07 in Resurgent U.S.," May 1, 2011, www.bloomberg.com.

30. Ibid.

31. Miriam Jordan, "Illegal Immigration from Mexico Hits Lowest Level in Decade," *Wall Street Journal,* July 23, 2006.

32. Starobin, "Dream Endangered."

33. Ibid.

34. Richard Florida, "Homeownership Is Overrated," *Wall Street Journal,* June 7, 2010.

35. The Gartman Letter, May 16, 2011.

36. Starobin, "Dream Endangered."

37. New Jersey Real Estate Report, "If You Are a Contrarian, Is It Time to Buy?" April 19, 2011, http://njrereport.com/index.php/2011/04/19/if-you-are-a-contrarian-is-it-time-to-buy/.

38. Lynch, "Phoenix's Underwater Mortgages."

Chapter 5   You Can't Handle the Truth, or the Volatility

1. John Maynard Keynes, *The General Theory of Employment, Interest and Money (2008 Edition).* (New Delhi: Atlantic Books, 2008), 141.

2. James Altucher, "10 Reasons You Should Never Own Stocks Again," April 29, 2011, www.businessinsider.com/10-reasons-you-should-never-own-stocks-again-2011-4.
3. James B. Stewart, "A Decade of Buying and Selling Stocks," June 13, 2011, www.smartmoney.com/invest/stocks/common-sense-success-a-decade-of-buying-and-selling-stocks-1307395134226/?link=SM_clm_sum.
4. Tracy Alloway, "Depression ★alert★," January 27, 2009, http://ftalphaville.ft.com/blog/2009/01/27/51728/depression-alert/.
5. Andy Kessler, *Eat People: And Other Unapologetic Rules for Game-Changing Entrepreneurs* (New York: Portfolio, 2011), location 1329.
6. Bob Davis, "Rise of Nationalism Frays Global Ties," April 28, 2008, www.dallariva.org/csumba/mba602/Sum08/Globalization%202.pdf.
7. David Smick, *The World Is Curved: Hidden Dangers to the Global Economy* (New York: Portfolio, 2008).

Chapter 6   Still the One

1. George Friedman, *The Next 100 Years: A Forecast for the 21st Century* (New York: Doubleday, 2009).
2. Larry Page interview, October 28, 2000, www.achievement.org/autodoc/page/pag0int-2.
3. Sergey Brin bio, www.businessinsider.com/blackboard/sergey-brin.
4. Jason Riley, *Let Them In* (New York, New York: Gotham, 2008), 65.
5. "Anybody Home?" *Wall Street Journal*, June 27, 2011.
6. "Working Class," *Wall Street Journal*, June 27, 2011.
7. Joseph Rago, "Tom Wolfe's Advice: Escape the 'Parenthesis States' and Explore America," *Wall Street Journal*, March 11, 2006.

Acknowledgments

I am indebted to my grammarian mother for teaching me to love language and to my high school English teacher, Jon Woodell, for teaching me to write. I will always appreciate my brother, Dennis Cortés, for teaching me about financial markets. To all the folks at CNBC, you make television fun and informative—special gratitude to Gary Kaminsky, Susan Krakower, John Melloy, Scott Wapner, Dennis Gartman, Melissa Lee, and Mary Duffy. Thanks to my agent, Jeffrey Krames, for getting me published, and to Emilie Herman at John Wiley & Sons for patiently guiding my manuscript. A huge shout-out to Tom Pahlke at Veracruz for invaluable assistance in researching. And most of all, always, much love to my family—my beautiful wife and treasured children—for tolerating my preoccupation with this project.

About the Author

STEVEN CONNOR CORTÉS has traded independently since 1998. In 2002, he founded Veracruz LLC, which provides real time market research to large institutional traders such as Wall Street broker/dealers, hedge funds, and sovereign wealth funds. He appears daily on CNBC as a contributor, primarily on *Fast Money*. He graduated in 1994 from Georgetown University, where he played football and was nominated by the university for a Rhodes Scholarship.

Index